CONTENTS

INTRODUCTION

Out sniffing the air, touching stuff, listening and watching, it's sometimes amazing…and lately dumbfounding. The stroll began decades ago, a start-from-zero effort to taste and understand life. It is a genuinely scientific inquiry, observing and trying to grasp and sort it out, watching people and watching human drama…and sometimes a clown show. Can't recall the show ever being as weird and wild as lately.

I doubt you remember anything from age two. I don't. But surely, we both learned stuff at that stage, because by nature we were curious about and tried to touch and taste everything. It's a good bet that by three we were better at extracting good and avoiding bad from the world around us than on the day we took our very first steps.

By six, like most kids, I knew about bees. They can sting. I knew you could get killed by a car, and I accepted adult wisdom on electricity. TV had cowboy shows, so I learned about dynamite. Somebody told me gasoline could explode, too, and I think probably every adult said don't breathe the fumes. I understood that grown-up-world demanded and would force me to go to school and sit at a desk and learn numbers and how to read. I mostly did as I was told.

Of course, almost all of us sometimes stray, not do exactly as we're told. We walk into trouble, do crazy stuff, laughable stuff, dangerous stuff. Some of it comes with the age (stage). Puberty to about 30 is especially good for that. Sex and cars drive some people nuts. Sadly, it's also when some get captured by booze and drugs. Crazy may be a little less visible in later decades, but there are no known age limits.

There is another dangerous thing. Philosophers and priests have been warning us about it forever. Those thinkers try to keep us from being led astray. I can't remember if there was a light-bulb moment, a flash of understanding, or whether some of the stories just slowly started to sink in, like the one about Moses coming down off the mountain and going into a rage when he found his Israelite followers worshiping a golden calf. Or maybe it was that James Bond thriller with him doing battle against his nemesis, the evil Goldfinger.

It was likely a more gradual revelation that slowly settled in my brain...that even more hazardous than cars and hormones is...**Money!** It's dangerous stuff, but we have to have it. We chase after it. Who among us hasn't stressed because we think we don't, or didn't, have enough?

A fortunate (probably small) minority recognize enough and kind of glide off the fast track. And some give careful thought to where to squirrel it when there is a bit of surplus. A few folks with a sense of humor watch the spectacle and laugh, because they quantify, and qualify, correctly. They laugh because they see the sometimes silliness of the chase and the absurdity that one member of the human tribe can have a thousand pairs of shoes...or a million pairs of shoes.

Regular folks are starting to get wise, though. When there's not enough for shoes, and a hoodie when the weather turns cold, the grumbling starts. Many times in the past, the guys with a thousand pairs didn't hear the discontent until it was too late. Students of history worry that we are close to a repeat of the too late, a violent leveling that spares injury to no one. There is a pretty broad consensus that the haves now have too much, and the have-nots are struggling. There's a growing consensus, too, that lunacy may have infected some among the haves near the top. It's getting wild.

CHAPTER 1

CHINA WON. A SHORT HISTORY.

A short history

But a century before China won, the United States won. And before that Europe was ahead of the rest. But then Europe decided to fight...itself. In the centuries before about 1900, it was almost continuous war. Millions died and workers built weapons instead of goods for the good life and a surplus for investment. America stayed out of it. Instead, the US invested and built, especially after the end of its own Civil War. By the beginning of World War One, The Great War, the United States was a rising economic giant. When it entered the war as an ally of Great Britain, France, and Russia, Germany's attempt to dominate was doomed. America had an extraordinary economy that could supply manpower and every other need at a pace that overwhelmed the war-ravaged one of Germany.

The short version of history after the war was that the boys came home to a frenzy of success, thanks to cheap energy, new technology, and plenty of land. Everybody could have a car and electricity in their home. In the roaring twenties the money flowed and accumulated, and quite a lot of it fell into the hands of speculators.

In Florida it was a land sales frenzy that preceded the stock market. Scammers followed the money. Even convicted felon Charles Ponzi tried to get in on it, convincing very-small-time investors to give him ten bucks for a house lot in a development "close to Jacksonville." Turned out each lot was one of 23 on an acre of land and many of the acres were swampy, where nobody would build. Ponzi was late, probably delayed by having to wait until his release from prison, so he turned out to be a bit player in the story.

The Florida bubble burst, due at least in part to a familiar combination of you know what "in the punchbowl." Interest rates, hurricanes, and insurance, shut down the party.

Florida portended what would follow in the stock market. Collapse of the land sale pyramid was an omen ignored. And then the really big bubble did burst, and the Great Depression followed.

Meanwhile, Europe was not settled. The population suffered extended hardship, not surprising considering the destruction of its built environment and massive loss of members of the would-be rebuilder workforce, to death and battlefield injury. Europe was ripe for the message of scapegoating monsters like Hitler and Mussolini.

The US slowly climbed out of its economic trench, but unlike Europe it didn't have to first clear debris. The Great War didn't leave destruction on American soil. Here everything didn't have to be rebuilt, so there was money to invest in new things. That lack of experience of the destruction and the awfulness, up close, also probably partially explains why big money wasn't diverted to spending on weapons until after the Japanese attack on Pearl Harbor.

Because much more of the American surplus was invested rather than being required for cleanup and the military during the two decades between WWI and WWII, a latently solid economy was available for a quick and vigorous response to the attack by the Japanese. Very shortly after Pearl Harbor that economy joined the European effort to stop the Nazis. America had deep resources at the ready.

The Allies won, albeit only after release on Japan of the new weapon that would, and continues to terrorize the world, the atomic bomb. The United States declared itself the leader of the world. In most places there was agreement on that.

Germany and Japan were defeated, but there was one other place where one other stubborn power player fairly quickly didn't agree, Russia. Joseph Stalin, a dictator some believed to be just as brutal and homicidal as Hitler, was still in power, and he hadn't surrendered anything. The Russian war-years experience was awful. Millions died. Some claimed that much of the mass death was at Stalin's hands. But he was still in power, and soon he and the Soviet Union also had the bomb.

Americans were told it was freedom, our side, against imprisonment by the Communists on the other. The Communist Party was the international plot trying to take over the world. This was the start of the Cold War, a war with no shooting, just pointing hundreds, or thousands, of weapons at each other, some capable of killing, vaporizing, most every living thing within a hundred miles of where it hit.

By many measures it was a bi-polar world. Certainly, that was the case for military power. The Soviets and the United States spent huge sums on weapons. We spent money on intercontinental ballistic missiles tipped with megaton nuclear warheads, and submarines and aircraft carriers. We maintained armies. The US and Russia spent. Germany and Japan weren't allowed to. They repaired and then they invested. Both of those countries were technologically advanced before the war. And they had educated populations.

In the 1950s and early 1960s, "made in Japan" meant cheap. Flimsy metal kids' toys often had a "Made in Japan" label.

That was about the time we started seeing weird little cars called Volkswagens, from Germany. They could go a lot more miles on a gallon of gas, and their rear engine made them better in the snow.

By the mid-seventies, Japanese televisions were as good as anybody's, and there were Volkswagens in every neighborhood along with some BMWs, Volvos, and Saabs. And then came a trickle of cars from Japan. Those were small and not fancy or super fun, but they didn't break down, and they just cost less to drive than the standard fare from America's "big-three" establishment.

By the mid-eighties the trickle was a flood, and it was all over but the shouting for the worldwide dominance of American car companies. Everybody was in a Toyota or Honda or wheels from Germany.

German goods, though slightly more expensive, were understood to be the highest quality available from anywhere, including the United States.

The Cold War ended because Russia couldn't keep up. Smart as its scientists and engineers were at matching the United States, or racing ahead in space and in building weapons, the Soviet economy was too small. And the Russians, just like the US, had for decades been spending on their military rather than investing.

Mikhail Gorbachev, the Russian president, announced glasnost (opening) and perestroika (restructuring). Gorbachev and our President Reagan shook hands, and the Soviet Union broke up in 1991. Senator Paul Tsongas of Massachusetts, campaigning for president in 1992, succinctly explained the ending. "The Cold War is over; Japan won."[1]

That's ancient history for half of America. The irony of the end of the Cold War is probably missed. Maybe it wasn't an ending anyway, more like just the end of a chapter, and the story continues. When Tsongas made that astute observation in 1992 our country was still sore from the embarrassment of failure in Vietnam. We needed a win, and Reagan delivered. He was worshiped in some quarters, because though the Russians were given a dignified, warm, welcome, it felt like a win for us. We won, and then there was a calm. But the calm didn't last, and the momentary possibility of reducing spending on weapons and restoring investment didn't last.

Petro-state (Iraq) dictator Saddam Hussain, aggrieved by activity in the oil fields shared with his neighbor Kuwait, decided the remedy was invasion. USA proclaimed that a threat to world peace and stability and chased the bully back to his home turf, Iraq. Then American warplanes controlled the skies above and kept him down, and oil flowed okay. There was obvious need to keep up the US defense budget.

At the same time Washington became even more friendly to speculators, though it claimed its policies were rewarding investors. Germany and Japan continued to gain market share, and other places, like Taiwan and South Korea, started to be players in the manufacture of modern things, notably electronics. It looked like the world was progressing.

On September 11, 2001, Osama bin Laden's suicide volunteers on hijacked airliners put a shock ending to any sense of tranquility when they tried to take out the money capital of the world by taking down its twin towers, and with another plane putting a hole in America's iconic fort, The Pentagon. They killed 3,000 Americans. Their attacks took us down for days, and even now,

25 years later, keep us nervous and inconvenienced with security checks routine in almost any place that could conceivably be a future target.

The attackers made it clear the United States was no longer a safe island protected by vast oceans and friends immediately on the other side of its northern and southern borders. America went to war again...on terror. It wasn't a time to cut defense spending and invest, although revenue (tax) cuts and their claimed benefits were still okay. Tax cuts were by then almost religious dogma. Investment was off the table because resources had to be spent on the fight, and you can only borrow so much money.

The terrorists had weapons of mass destruction, WMDs, we were told. Tragic character of our time, Colin Powell, then Secretary of State, who was a respected leader who might have eventually retired from service to the country as President, disgraced himself when he presented the WMD lie to the United Nations Security Council in order to get its blessing for what was to come next, war against Iraq.

There was a lot of oil in Iraq and neighboring Iran, but as it turned out, no WMDs, at least not in Iraq. None of the hijackers who crashed planes into the World Trade Center and Pentagon were Iraqis. 15 of the 19 hijackers were from Saudi Arabia. Bin Laden, a Saudi, was hiding in the mountains of Afghanistan and directing his war from there. America entered a quagmire again. The Afghanistan part would last for twenty years, with the end sadly reminiscent of its predecessor debacle in Vietnam.

Meanwhile, goods from Asia got increasingly plentiful for consumers on this side of the globe. Cisco Systems, a giant in the internet buildout, and other big companies bought components from China. More and more products at Walmart had a "made in China" stamp, and names like LG, Samsung, and Lenovo wedged in on Sony, Dell, and Apple. And all the while, American "investors" pushed the manufacture of American brands to Mexico, and they demanded more tax cuts. They refused to acknowledge, or pretended ignorance of, the necessity of investment in infrastructure and in the skills and health of the home workforce.

Those same players with money did respond and start to build when the government handed out money, as was the case briefly when the Biden administration was able to open the purse strings to upgrade dilapidated old public goods, like roads and bridges, and also to build needed new infrastructure, for example, production lines for computer chips and infrastructure that will speed the transition away from fossil fuels.

The political will to invest was in place for a moment following the economic plunge caused by the COVID-19 pandemic. Government policy fueled investment, but the window of opportunity closed quickly, and projects that didn't complete in that moment stalled.

As always, there are losers when a new paradigm pushes away an old one. Fossil fuel interests had, and have, severe losses in their future because successor technology is just so much better and cheaper. The fossil fuelers have reason to try to manipulate everything. In 2024 they very rationally used their push to help elect a president who claims the new paradigm is completely a hoax. The speculators don't care. China may be happy.

Perhaps "China won" is an overstatement. Maybe nobody ever wins but rather just grabs the lead for a while. It's a good bet that the US is not winning at the moment. Decades of underinvestment in education and technology, energy technology especially, and very high defense spending assures us of higher costs and lower productivity.

In addition to continued expense for weapons, we pay nearly double for health care, and based on cost trends and current real costs for renewables and batteries for transportation, our holding on to old technology energy spending is and will be a significant drag relative to our competitors. Together a 15% handicap compared to the leaders is a hard to challenge estimate. In 2026 and looking forward, Americans can anticipate a standard of living that declines relative to our peers. Ours is not a good trajectory. China moves ahead.

---

[1] https://quotefancy.com/quote/1449247/Paul-Tsongas-The-cold-war-is-over-Japan-won

CHAPTER 2

CHINA SYNDROME AGAIN.

Not fiction this time.

In 1979 a movie, "The China Syndrome"[1] with Jack Lemmon, Jane Fonda, and Michael Douglas won praise at the Cannes Film Festival and then went on to make huge money for Columbia Pictures. The story line was a nuclear runaway, a reactor meltdown all the way...to China, on the other side of the earth. The film's timing was amazing, released just 12 days before the real thing at Three Mile Island, right next to Harrisburg, Pennsylvania. That accident was a major setback for the industry and a scary time for the neighborhood and neighbors, including my own family and friends about 35 miles downwind.

The TMI site, after many years lying idle, is to open again with its undamaged other reactor brought back online, thanks to a planned $16 billion joint effort by Microsoft and Constellation Energy. It will serve the power-hungry AI industry.

The catastrophic possibility in the movie, that molten radioactive metal and everything encasing it, would accelerate down, down, down, pulled to the center of the earth by extreme gravity and then blasted up and out the other side in China, was science fiction at its best.

Today there's another stressful China story, and it's not fiction. Now it's a different kind of runaway, not liquid metal. It is runaway in both directions, a massive movement of goods on a semicircle on the surface of the earth to the US, and then going the other way, money through the ether to a satellite and then in a nanosecond back to earth on the other side. There's handwringing over China's trade surplus that was more than a trillion dollars in 2025. Donald Trump accuses China of cheating to make its stuff cheap. He says the Chinese manipulate their currency. They keep the renminbi (yuan) undervalued, and that means the dollar in comparison is too high. Americans can buy more with their dollars, but Chinese consumers can't buy what we make because their currency is weak. Is it so?

Inflation.

One marker, inflation rate, might offer a clue. Currency manipulation usually means pumping up the supply, printing more of it, inflating it.

People understand that inflation generally results in having to pay more dollars for something this time than they did the last time. In China, inflation would mean pay more in renminbi. If the government is manipulating your currency to keep it cheap, inflating it, you probably will have to fork over more of the bills in your wallet the next time you buy something. If the Chinese government is guilty and our own isn't, higher inflation there would be an indicator.

It turns out the evidence points in the opposite direction from the president's claim. The inflation rate, in the time period since the China colossus started to take off about 20 years ago, has been running about twice as high here, lately around 3% but only about 1.5% over there. That suggests weaker purchasing power for Americans and relatively more for the Chinese. It would seem their currency, because of government policy or something else, is getting stronger compared to ours. Mr. Trump has it backwards.

But the President has a point in bemoaning the fact that so many of the goods of our everyday life travel 10,000 miles on a ship and then a bunch more by truck before they're delivered to our house...instead of being made here by you and me and our neighbors down the street.

Tariffs or slave labor?

If it isn't currency manipulation what else might explain the Amazon phenomenon, now at the end of the first quarter of the 21st century, and before that, Walmart? How is it that all those things we buy, the made in China ones, are usually the best buy for the money, even with the cost of long-distance transportation included? Could it be tariffs? Or slave labor on a massive scale? Could it be China has 800 million indentured servants who barely survive on bread and water, or just rice?

Blaming tariffs for making goods cheap is exactly backwards. A tariff raises the price of something you buy at Walmart. If somebody in China bought something made here and there was a tariff added as it entered that country, they would pay more. Nope, we don't get cheap stuff because China collects tariffs.

China has been accused of human rights abuses. Ethnic Uyghurs in China's western mountain interior have been abused according to many reports. There have been accusations of forced labor. One Australian study[2] offered the number 80,000 from the Xinjian region who have been trained (or force-trained) and then sent to other provinces to work. The Chinese Government denies that it is slave labor or rights abuse. Their alternative description of government action is that it is a necessary remedy for social unrest and a curb on religious extremism.

Most of the world doesn't completely buy that explanation, but it probably doesn't view it as a humanitarian crisis on the same scale as what has happened in Gaza, or earlier episodes of mass cruelty throughout human history, either.

But what about that notion that the action does keep stuff cheap, so cheap that American producers can't compete? Is it those abused Uyghurs who are keeping prices low and giving China unfair advantage? Slightly less abusive than slavery, might it be indentured servitude on a mass scale?

That is officially illegal in China. It is in the United States, too. But in both places, there seem to always be some employers who will exploit workers any time there is opportunity to do so. Law enforcement tries to limit the abuse, but low skilled workers especially, or ones with less than perfect credentials, do sometimes suffer. That the term isn't used much by the crowd that is now happy to blame China for every one of America's ills, suggests the data really is lacking that would show the 800,000,000 members of the Chinese workforce are in some kind of bondage. To put it into perspective, too, some point out that many American workers feel trapped. Uncertain healthcare accessibility, absent a tie to an employer, is surely a mobility inhibitor for many. And non-compete clauses and NDAs certainly constrain some creative individuals.

A recent example of corporate muscling of employees is recounted by Sarah Wynn-Williams, in her book Careless People.[3] As a high-level employee of a social media company, she learned on leaving it that she and others who believed themselves to be multi-millionaires, by virtue of claim to shares in that company, only had claim while they remained tied to it. Leave by choice, or not choice, and you leave the shares behind.

Stolen intellectual property.

Chinese people are industrious and skilled. By most estimates the country's universities award a million and a half or more engineering degrees every year, about seven times as many as the US. The number of new PhDs in engineering and math is about equal to the number of Uyghurs believed to have been sent away as unwilling laborers. China has succeeded in developing and continues to develop a deep well of talent. Those talented people work. They are creative, even though detractors claim the top-down system of rules doesn't allow room for genuine innovation.

For a long time, the detractors said it was simply the copying of western intellectual property, pirating it, that explained extraordinary economic performance. Also, they continue to point out the China success record started from a very depressed base.

Manufacturing competence, clearly evidenced by the cost per unit for superior quality and performance goods, regardless of the source of the intelligence built into those goods, is essential. Intellectual property theft is an inadequate argument.

China Syndrome2 is real. But it isn't a story of America being left in the dust because the competition cheats by manipulating its money or that people in China are enslaved and working for crumbs. It isn't true either that every invention or discovery in science and technology happens in the west and is then stolen. Overlooked by the critics especially, there is one additional essential ingredient for economic success, investment.

Investment.

China has invested in people and in infrastructure. It now has a modern transportation system that, when compared side by side with the one of the US, makes much of the latter's nearly century of wear and rust and insufficient spending on necessary maintenance quite obvious.

It has built factories that are so efficient at turning out solar panels and batteries that they undercut those produced almost everywhere else in the world. Levelized cost of energy, solar electric energy, in the range of $.03/kWh[4] is becoming the norm, while best case scenario in the United States is probably double that. In many regions of the US electricity costs $.15/kWh to generate with natural gas and $.30/kWh delivered to your house.

Because motor drive batteries produced in China now cost less than $100/kWh, very capable electric cars are the choice of more than half of buyers because some are available for $20,000. Those low-cost batteries, if configured for stationary storage can nearly eliminate the intermittency issue that is inherent with wind and solar electricity.

Regardless of the exact mix of factors that power the flood of Chinese goods, the American consumer is being denied some of the benefit. We are not getting as big a share of the payback from China's earlier investment. We can't buy a $15,000 or $20,000 EV because our own government is prohibiting their entry into the country. A quite capable, but not very many bells and whistles vehicle is not available here at that price. We can't easily get the low-cost solar panels, either. Whether or not tariffs, imposed for the stated purpose of protecting American workers, ultimately do stimulate production at home and generate new jobs, for now it is a loss to consumers. Either we just don't receive as much of the flow of the goods, or we pay more.

---

[1] https://a.co/d/0gXYVZc4 - China Syndrome movie on Amazon

[2] https://www.uyghuraa.org/reports/forcedlabour?utm_source=chatgpt.com

[3] https://us.macmillan.com/books/9781250391230/carelesspeople/

[4] https://www.pv-tech.org/solar-pv-retains-most-competitive-lcoe-globally-in-2025-wood-mackenzie/

CHAPTER 3

MONEY-OIL-WILD!

Method or madness?

Isn't it strange, that list of places where our Mr. Trump is most eager to engage? And drop bombs, Iran being the latest target. That "little excursion" is apparently going to cost taxpayers a couple hundred billion dollars, what the Pentagon says it needs in a supplemental appropriation.[1] Before that, Venezuela got a dose of Trump attention that killed a couple hundred people as its president was whisked away. And kind of ancient history now, there was that Christmas Day gift for Nigeria.

Russia, Qatar, Iran, and Venezuela grab his attention. In Nigeria it was supposedly in defense of Christians.

Qatar? They gave our president a big jet. The super-lux B747 was estimated to be worth $400 million. Some airplane folks think it's obsolete, and some critics say, "Who cares about gold toilets and drapes or whatever other, maybe dated, symbols of opulence are inside?" The story has pretty much disappeared since Spring 2025 when the bird landed in USA to start its reconfiguration as an Air Force One. The President's style is to sometimes lavish gifts, like pardons, on others, and he does accept them, too. $400 million is a pretty nice token of appreciation from a little country of just over 3 million people. We number more than 300 million.

Russia is a different story, a bit of love-hate. It looked like a budding bromance, that early meeting in Alaska. Or maybe it wasn't budding, but rather a continuation of the one in Helsinki during a previous presidential iteration. Thanks to the Alaska understanding, the war would soon be over in Ukraine, not quite on Trump's first day in office, but it seemed Putin was starting to be reasonable and work with his American counterpart...the peacemaker. Like the big jet, haven't heard much about this success story recently, either. Many months have passed, and missiles and drones are still destroying buildings and ships and killing people.

Our country's relationship with Iran has been awful for decades. Iran gets blamed, maybe correctly, for a lot of the ongoing mess with its neighbors, some of whom we consider our friends. Iranians meddle, and they seem to want to build their own nukes. They really don't like Israel and Saudi Arabia, and the feeling is mutual. Trump sent planes all the way from continental US to drop really-big-bang bunker-buster bombs and then claimed to have completely obliterated Iran's deeply hidden nuclear weapons effort. Later evaluation of the damage suggests the claim was a bit overstated. Turns out, it wasn't the end of the story, maybe more like a footnote in the ongoing craziness show.

The Iran situation is a mess and has been a mess off and on for decades, going back at least to the 1950s when our CIA overthrew the elected leader and propped up a king (shah) and dictator more to our liking. The elected president, a guy named Mohammad Mossadegh made the mistake of telling the world that the oil in Iran belonged to Iranians. Interests in the UK and US had a different opinion.

The Shah, Mohammad Reza Pahlavi, ruled for more than twenty years, in an often-glamorous style and often with brutal enforcement of his authority by the hated SAVAK secret police force. Iran was on our side in the Middle East push and pull and against others aligned with the Soviet Union in the Cold War.

A year into his term, Jimmy Carter made the fatal political mistake of traveling to Tehran and embracing a clearly unpopular and declining Shah. The president called Iran an "Island of Stability."[2] Based on events that followed, it's pretty clear that Carter's words on New Year's Eve 1977 sealed the fate if his presidency.

In 1979, America's "friend," in ill health, ran away, and the clerics took over. They held Americans hostage in the U.S. Embassy until after our presidential election. It was a humiliating experience for most Americans. Carter was punished at the polls for his mistake, and the hostages were released as Ronald Reagan assumed the office.

Today the clerics, or whoever is actually in charge, are struggling after the Supreme Leader, an obviously very old man, was taken out by another round of Israeli and U.S. bombing strikes. Well before the U.S. overt action there was discontent in the streets, with thousands killed in a forceful ongoing putdown of rebellion as the Iranian power elite attempt to stay in power. Old (not quite as old) man Trump attacked, so he said, because there was failure to bow to his terms regarding the nuclear weapons development...which he previously claimed to have destroyed. The Iranians said they would negotiate, but in a display of stubbornness perhaps, conducted military exercises that disrupted shipping. That was enough to bump the price of oil up 10%, in hindsight barely a ripple for the market.

The whole area now, and for how long nobody knows, is a war zone with drones and bombs and bullets flying in both directions.

The Strait of Hormuz is closed…or open, and a fifth of the world's oil flow is cut off…or not. With sunken ships and mines in that channel, it's not surprising that the price of crude has spiked up. It could be a new price plateau, not just a spike, at about double the December 2025 low. Some observers see a hundred bucks a barrel as an intermediate price with the longer-term plateau considerably higher. Considering the stubbornness of the clerics in Iran, the bitter determination of Netanyahu in Israel, and the chaos of Trump, it's doubtful anyone is making predictions with confidence. Maybe an unintended consequence for whoever is writing or directing this money story is that the oil part of it is suddenly much more visible.

After the first bombs in the mountains of Iran, what seemed like ancient history just three months later, the US was on to Venezuela. Our president, who is well known to exaggerate...and lie, and clearly enjoys stirring things up, says we are under attack by "narcoterrorists," and they're coming from Venezuela. The president of that country, Nicolas Maduro was accused of being the leader of the gang.

The two presidents reportedly talked on the phone. There was speculation on the possibility of a deal. That seemed quite plausible since either one of them would, and has, done deals with the devil. No certainty in this conversation which dealer is which.

It's an ugly scene that three days into the new year (2026) got decidedly uglier. US military strikes on small boats with a lot of people dying, seizure of ships loaded with oil, in international waters, all in the name of the American People, and then added was a kidnapping. Our president ordered the bombing of the capital of the country and the kidnapping of its president.

President Trump at a press conference said "We're going to run the country..." According to NBC News, Trump said the U.S. will temporarily "run" Venezuela and work to tap the country's massive oil reserves.[3]

His press conference included this: *In his remarks, Trump said that U.S. oil companies were prepared to make major investments in the country. "We're going to have our very large United States oil companies, the biggest anywhere in the world, go in, spend billions of dollars, fix the badly broken infrastructure, the oil infrastructure, and start making money for the country," he said.* Money-oil-crazy! At least it would be…in normal times.

Of course, all presidents engage with the rest of the world. We want them to. This one has had pissing contests with some, like our neighbors immediately north and south. And he's poked the giant Asian bear, er...dragon, with tariffs. That hasn't gone particularly well, maybe because Dragonland (China) is as big as the US and has four times as many people. The dragon sort of smiled and said no. The "no!" softened slightly. And then there was a whisper back to Mr. T. "We'll play along for a bit, but you know we're going to win."

Long-time observers of Donald Trump know he's a showman, a carnival barker. They haven't been surprised that the show continues. Even his performance at Davos wasn't unexpected. It was embarrassing, but quite in character. What looks like "crazy" is part of it. Some skeptics think there's more to the enterprise, maybe pickpockets cruising through the audience while the show goes on. But the skeptics, the non-believers, and there are more and more of us, understand the methods, "flood the zone" or "just throw everything against the wall and see what sticks."

Jet fuel perhaps?

It has become clear there's something else at play. It's not just the Trump show and China winning. Russia, Iran, Venezuela and the Davos insults hurled at Europe, at first glance seems a chaos random puzzle. Could it be there is some "real thing" hidden in that dust storm? Jet fuel, maybe? Russia has natural gas, more than anybody else. The US has it, too, but we're way down at number four,[4] with about a fourth as much as Russia. Guess who's number two. Iran. And in third place is little Qatar, not many people and a big old jet, and gas.

Oil is interesting and becomes more so by the day, or hour. Venezuela, where Trump would have you believe drug running is the main business, has more oil than anybody. It's even more than Saudi Arabia, home to our president's new best buddy (according to some accounts). In third place? Iran. US made the top ten, but barely, at number nine just behind Russia.[5] There does seem to be an "engagement" connection here, an association. Wells.

On that account, the Christmas episode initially seemed a bit outside the lines. Brutality at the hands of ISIS is well documented, and it seems Christians in Nigeria are victims of it, as are Muslims. Mr. Trump says the US sent missiles to put an end to Christian suffering.

Reports from the area are limited, so the extent of damages from the American military action are speculative. Were people killed, or because it is a sparsely populated region was damage limited to destruction of a small barn or two and loss of a few goats? Bombing and probably killing people on Christmas Day in the name of the American People and invoking the name of Christ as justification? Really? Was Christian suffering what this was about?

Or could it be...going back to the conspiracy theory window into the story, that other thing sometimes hidden but so often lurking? Oil?

The dots are harder to connect on this one. Nigeria is a major oil producer, but relations with the United States are generally okay, so that fact, the oil, is unnoticed most of the time. Also, Nigeria is a big country, the largest in Africa. The oil and gas producing regions are in the southeastern part. The US air strikes were in the remote northwest. How could it be about oil? Maybe it's not oil from Nigeria.

Bordering Nigeria to the north is the country of Niger. Until recently oil produced in Niger was essentially just enough for domestic consumption, the country being a minor producer. Apparently, nobody thought there was very much additional of that resource hidden under a barren, hot, dry landscape. Recently however, studies likely motivated by Chinese interests, reveal a large reserve, perhaps a billion barrels or more. A new pipeline opened in 2024 carries that oil to an Atlantic port in Benin twelve hundred miles away. The port facilities there can load a million barrels a day, about the same output as Venezuela. The pipeline runs from wells in eastern Niger, westerly, roughly parallel to the border with Nigeria before making a turn south into Benin. On a big map,[6] that line looks like it would require just a few degrees course correction to make it a target for the Tomahawks that struck Sokoto State in northwest Nigeria, officially in response to atrocities against Christians.

Oh, and just in! There's oil in Kazakhstan,[7] a bunch more (maybe 25 times as much) than Niger, and it's closer to a port. The flow is slow, though, partly because it goes through the war zone in Russia. Ukraine keeps trying to blow up the pipes. Folks in Kazakhstan, including consortium partner Chevron, have invested almost $50 billion and want to pump that oil.

This is a chaotic mess puzzle. Donald Trump is clearly a factor but is he the real agent or just the role player handy to stir the pot when needed, or maybe distract? His comments after Maduro's abduction suggest he might not be the ideal character actor this time. If his lines were supposed to divert our attention away from oil, he completely blew it. He said the US was going to "run" the place, dictate in Venezuela...and pump oil. Really big US oil companies will exploit a really big underground lake of oil.

There's room for a bit of skepticism here because of another interesting marker, the price of crude. A long-term trend line, say from 1975, would suggest an inflation-adjusted price today of about $85/barrel. The actual auction price had lately been sticky at $60. Surplus, maybe? ***Too much*** oil already? And the Chinese are trying to flood the whole world with their cheap EVs and solar panels. What happens when a couple of billion people realize they don't need oil?

Meanwhile in Dragonland.

In Dragonland, where there isn't as much of that honey from the deep, half of all new cars run on batteries, and electricity harvested directly from sunshine is cheap. And it's a place with a lot of smart, hardworking people. There are nearly 500 times as many in China as in Qatar. They're happy to drive on electricity and see at night with light provided by solar energy stored in batteries rather than gas from Qatar, or oil from Saudi Arabia, or Venezuela.

Some of those electric cars, that are good enough to keep lots of the world's drivers happy for about $20,000, are manufactured in Brazil. Chinese tech has escaped way beyond its borders, beyond its hemisphere. And that's true if you measure hemisphere east-west or north-south.

The Chinese export and expand and build, and they import oil. They still have a lot of gasoline powered vehicles and not so many wells. They invest around the world. We might have imagined Xi whispering in Maduro's ear while Trump was thinking his offer...the one that you can't refuse...was a done deal. It could have been those rusting Venezuelan wells and refineries getting refurbished by the Chinese and then having that huge underground reserve released onto the market. World price plunge to $30, or even lower if investors decided risk to a pipeline from a new bounty in Niger was acceptably low. Some guys in West Texas and Saudi Arabia would starve. Well maybe not Saudi Arabia. Students of the subject think Saudis wells may still be viable at $20. They cite a bit of not so ancient Middle East history.

In the early 1970s when a newly empowered tyrant named Muammar Gaddafi in Libya told the world the oil there belonged to Libyans and that they would get paid for it, the Iraqis, Iranians and Saudis suddenly realized they had been practically giving it away. Before Gaddafi talked back to the western establishment, the Saudis had been pumping and selling oil for less than $2/barrel.[8] Adjusted for inflation, that would be about $10 in 2026.

Off the table.

Of course, now that line of speculation (the whisper theory) is off the table. Trump claims, or did a couple months ago, to be in charge in Venezuela, so apparently it won't be Chinese engineers and technicians bringing the oil infrastructure back to life there. American oil companies will be on it instead. Or will they?

There are a couple of possibilities here. Unlikely would be a genuine competitive scramble among the fossil fuel giants. Production now, despite it being the world's largest reserve, is very low, probably a little less than 1% of total world output. A scramble with the major players trying to outdo each other at grabbing that oil reserve and selling it would be suicidal. A supply flood would trigger a price crash that kills everybody.

But there will have to be some claim of success. Trump will need to be able to say he was right in taking over, and the oil boys need to keep him in office in order to slow the inevitable, a plug in the well...thanks to Chinese central planning and the developed technology of batteries and solar panels.

As chaotic as it looks, the Trump part in the bigger story, the chaos feature, may be part of the plan, keeping the rest of us a bit uncertain of our own sanity. If you're a news junkie you've likely had days when, because of the chaos, a calmed mind requires closing the screen and going for a walk in the woods. "Can't make this shit up" keeps popping into the consciousness.

Acknowledgement of the oil in Trump's January news conference sounded like a blunder, but maybe it wasn't. It could be the script, and he is the right character actor for the script at this moment. Exxon and company could put a coat of paint on the rusting refineries and then bump up production by 50% or even 100% and hand over some beautiful photoshopped images and bragging rights to the president. Exxon could easily offset the increase by reducing production from a marginal field or two someplace else in the world, and the markets wouldn't even blink. Trump would claim to have doubled production, Americans probably wouldn't notice that the price at the pump hadn't dropped from $4.50 to $2.50, and the Cuban expats who heard threats to Cuba in that meandering press conference would probably still be happy. And of course, Venezuelan expats also in Florida would continue cheering wildly.

"Just joking" on that $2.50 a gallon for gasoline, and hey, early 2026 is ancient history, anyway. With the Strait of Hormuz closed and none of the guys with ships and guns willing or able to open it up, $4.50 is the new reality. It will be a hundred bucks a week to drive the family F250 instead of half that. Some of the MAGA faithful must be a bit disappointed. Surely the strategic thinkers in the oil business aren't exactly comfortable, either. With that price maybe shooting up too high too quickly, you have to wonder if some observers with a calmed mind might recognize a "dog caught the car" moment.

Brazil?

Brazil? You probably noticed it was added to the mix a couple paragraphs back. The biggest headline story there was Jair Bolsonaro, the former president who tried to copy our Jan 6th event but didn't get away with it, going to prison. It was a failed coup and so was Donald Trump's attempt to rescue his friend from the Brazilian criminal justice system.

Other news from that major western hemisphere country tells of the Chinese building BYD (Build Your Dreams) EVs there. And we're told the country's now-president is showing interest in also joining the top oil producer's club. With a gusher on the coast of Brazil, could the surplus become a flood? Can you imagine the really big players in the world-wide fossil fuel cartel ***not*** being "engaged" with a strategy to prevent that? Energy is an almost $10 trillion a year business, a river of money probably bigger than any other in human history. At $25 a barrel, the game would be all over for most of its players.

Maybe it's all over already, and they know it. Those Chinese panels and batteries can deliver electric miles at the equivalent of about $1.50/gallon. The US Energy Information Administration, EIA, says the crude oil to produce a gallon of motor fuel accounts for about half the total cost at retail. That would be $1.50 when it sells for $3 bucks at the pump. Simple math tells you that if oil sells at $63 for a 42-gallon barrel, you have it (the raw material) at $1.50 per gallon. That means the everything-else cost, like refining and transportation to get it to your tank is also $1.50. How can they, the oil producers, compete with batteries at a dollar fifty when their everything-else cost for a gallon of gasoline is $1.50? You the consumer would have to pay that even if the price of the crude oil fell to zero.

The short answer: Maybe you, the producer, don't compete. Truth be told, maybe you never did; could be competition was a myth, fake. For the rest of us, ever hear of OPEC? Manipulation, maybe?

If you're in the oil business your strategy now has to be to just hold on...the old-fashioned way, cheat. You hire politicians, and they write the rules, and the rules send the money your way, even if the free-market auction says your stuff is too expensive.

You have your guys impose tariffs on the lower cost new technology. You might even tighten the oil market by sabotaging or even bombing competitors who could also supply it. Do you suppose anybody ever considered taking out (down) the oil production from Venezuela? Oh...has the largest reserves but produces a meager 1 million barrels a day, while Saudi Arabia does 10 and USA 13. Hmm...

Back to the sleepy president and his attention span. Venezuela, Russia, Saudi Arabia, Iran, Brazil, Qatar, Nigeria...or maybe

Niger; they get noticed. Before the election the oil guys got noticed, and they got notice: "Contribute a billion dollars to my campaign." Whether it was said explicitly or not, everybody in the room understood the deal. "Get me elected, and I'll blow up all the Biden initiatives that would speed the transition to the new energy paradigm." In light of news a third of the way into this president's term it sure looks like a deal made, a deal honored. The amount was a pittance for that Mar-a-Lago audience, pocket change, but the right token at the right time.

Having a friend back in the White House is a big deal for the fossil fuelers, but what about for Trump? He's not an oil billionaire, doesn't own half the wells in Oklahoma...or Florida. Could it have something to do with that other part, that other part of the government called the legislative branch, where half the members come from states with significant oil and natural gas production? Alignment perhaps. Money keeps flowing to the oil boys, and Trump stays out of jail because the oil-boys-half of the house (House and Senate) won't call him out on anything. They won't do that because for a pittance the folks with the real money can and do keep them in office. Financing a campaign for a U.S. House seat may cost $10 million, beer money if you have a thousand million or ten thousand million.

Unfriend his banker?

If Trump captures your attention, no doubt there is one other of his fixations you've probably noticed. Confrontation with every competing authority, be it courts, or the opposing political party, or institutions of knowledge and research, and of course the media, is his norm. He attempts to run over every opponent.

One authority seems to annoy him even more than most, because he hasn't been able to run over it, the central bank, the Federal Reserve. He's repeatedly grumbled about its governing board chairman and even tried to fire members without cause. He blames The Fed for throttling his would-be great economy. Fed chair, Jerome Powell, was threatened, but by most indications, just kept doing his job, calling balls and strikes. He and his board wouldn't agree to pump up the money supply to goose the economy, plausibly a needed ointment for injury inflicted by tariffs and a government revenue shortfall triggered by tax cuts in the "Big Beautiful Bill" that was rammed through Congress at Trump's insistence. Trump demands way lower interest rates, but the "bond vigilantes" and other sober heads say, "no, no, no, inflation." *"Bond vigilantes" is a finance-world term for the wise (vigilant) ones, the responsible money guys who traditionally rail against the irresponsible spenders, the Democrats and their giveaways, especially. The vigilantes demand higher interest rates to loan to the government when it is spending too much of the money.*

Economists generally agree that added tariffs by themselves are inflationary. After the president's, what looked like pretty "wild-eyed" initial demands, in some cases a tax on imports of more than 100%, the actual incremental added cost to Americans for goods produced outside our borders has settled (maybe) at a more digestible level because the actual tariff rates imposed are much lower.

There isn't very solid agreement on how big an inflation increment has been added, but the data so far suggest there definitely is some increment. The calculated general inflation number has hovered just below 3%, about 50% higher than the Fed's target, and a little higher than the rate at the end of the Biden years.

So, inflation is running hotter than desired, and the president says print more money. Is this just more Trump madness or could there be some method? Could it be manifestation of habit, and we shouldn't be surprised? A punch in the face rather than a kiss is his habit, same for throwing his useful-idiot riders under the bus when they are no longer useful. But what other habit might be consistent, given what we know about the man's history, including his business history? Might it be that Trump understands money in a way that most of us don't usually consider. He made his money, and his kids are trying to do the same, in real estate.

Here's how that game (business) works: You use other people's money. And you don't pay taxes. You do have to put in some effort on things like recruiting tenants and occasionally replacing an aging roof or paving a parking lot. You manage the property and rent pays the bills. But the real money, what makes it worthwhile, comes courtesy of the calendar. It is time and inflation that produces the much bigger real gain, the real bang for your buck. Imagine you buy a building for $10 million and then 5 years later sell it for $15 million...a nice run-up because of inflation. That's especially true if you use other people's money.

Imagine your $10 million buy is with $1 million of your own and the rest borrowed. In this case you'd get a four to one return in five years. You've paid off your $9 million loan, and you now have $6 million in your pocket instead of $1 million.

Most likely it won't be quite that good. If inflation is 3%, like now, your sale price would be around $11.6 mil, your gain only 1.6, or 16% of the total purchase price. The thing is, there won't be any tax on your gain if you use the proceeds to purchase another property. Your next one can be bigger because you now have 2.6 to put into it, so maybe get a 26 million (the same 10 to 1 leverage) property.

There is one other very important factor here, how the IRS calculates income. It recognizes that most stuff, things that produce income, deteriorate with age. The thing loses some of its productive power. So, you are allowed to recognize that loss. You deduct depreciation from the cash flow you collect from your tenants. They pay you the full amount, but you report what's left after the depreciation expense. Imagine this scenario: Your tenants pay $2 million a year rent. You have some routine expenses, like electricity for lights in the common spaces, snow plowing, and an occasional visit by the plumber, and of course, property tax, total maybe $500,000. And you have a mortgage payment. It might be another $900,000. Assuming you're an honest businessperson and pay your bills, there will still be $600,000 left for you. But that's not what goes on the tax return. You subtract depreciation, which might be a million and a half...or two million. So, you owe nothing in taxes and will even have a tax loss to carry forward. You put groceries on the table, and if you're slightly frugal maybe have enough surplus to invest in...a boat maybe, if that's your fancy.

Back to Mr. Trump and his clan, the real estate bros. They know this game. They know the IRS can be unfriendly...and that it has muscle. They also know that inflation drives the price of fixed assets. Higher inflation means higher property values. If you have title to the real estate, you win. In the scenario above, with a 6% inflation rate, you would have about $4.4 million to invest at the start of your second round. You could end up with a $44 million building with your name on it five years after you started with a meager $1 million of your own money. Hmm...some interesting possibilities here if you're the boss of the government, or if he's just your close friend.

To make it even more interesting you might have your friend tear some muscle off the IRS to make it a little less of a pest and a little less nosey about accounting details and records. Then to really get things hoppin', replace the adults in the room at the Federal Reserve Board so it's on the same page to loosen the money supply, which it will then do. Here comes cheaper (and more) money. More available for real estate loans. And inflation takes off! Gives us pause, doesn't it? Mr. T. just a show with all those flood-the-zone antics? Maybe not. Might there be a plan, some real money here, too? Not just the oil. Hmm... Stay out of jail and some real money? Sounds like a plan, not pure chaos.

Plan or not, it is pretty wild and crazy. Some adults in the room worry that it's downright tippy.

---

[1] https://www.nytimes.com/2026/03/19/world/middleeast/pentagon-200-billion-iran-war-funding-hegseth.html

[2] https://www.politico.com/story/2018/12/30/this-day-in-politics-december-31-1077103

[3] https://www.nytimes.com/2025/12/05/business/energy-environment/venezuela-oil-trump.html?smid=url-share

[4] https://www.eia.gov/naturalgas/

[5] https://www.planete-energies.com/en/media/figures/global-natural-gas-reserves?utm_source=chatgpt.com

[6] https://www.gem.wiki/Niger–Benin_Oil_Pipeline

[7] A very large oil reservoir ready to pump https://www.nytimes.com/2026/01/03/business/chevron-kazakhstan-oil.html

[8] https://dspace.mit.edu/handle/1721.1/50146#:~:text=The%201970%20price%20of%20Saudi,tax%20increases%20raised%20the%20price.

CHAPTER 4

GRUNT. INVEST. SPECULATE.

Ballast to stay right side up.

We're starting to get wise though, to the crazy reality that this strobes and noise show and rocking the boat is according to plan, keeping us distracted as we try hard to not throw up. We're annoyed and a bit seasick but not completely incapacitated. We can still turn away from the latest flash and refocus.

Fireworks and chaos make it easier to hide stuff, like maybe the real oil-Trump-plan. Significant as that piece is, it's not the only story. There's one hiding behind it, maybe bigger than Iran, Venezuela, Greenland, Mexico and Canada combined, that matter of the billionaires having all the money and many of the rest of us scratching for a crumb. Some folks with a longer memory are worried the money is stacked to tippy heights. A tip-over would cause serious problems. And serious could be understatement, the disparity portending a much worse outcome, way worse than a fistful of dollars randomly scattering in the wind. Some of the hungry and disgruntled seem to have concluded they will never get their share, so might as well torch the stack and not even bother trying to tip it. They'd burn it all down. Probably ashes for my comfy little nest…and yours. Jan 6th, 2021, is a reminder.

Grunt.

Credit where credit is due, we would have nothing if nobody got their hands dirty, if nobody came home bone tired at the end of the day because their muscles or brains or both together had spent the day on the task of finding materials lying on the ground or scratching and drilling into the ground to extract them. And we'd have nothing if others weren't moving the stuff and separating the most important parts from the bulk. Most of us do our part...of the grunt work, all kinds of grunt work, teaching the kids, for example. Others grunt with the messes we make. Where we live would be pretty smelly and toxic if nobody was doing the clean-up. And we wouldn't have good stuff if some weren't hard at work manipulating the components, with math and microscopes at the start, and then with heat and pressure precisely applied. At every step there's a worker-bee watching, measuring, and intervening when needed to transform pieces of the earth around us and below us into things we now find essential to our comfort and survival. We absolutely need those manufactured things. And we need all of us, all the worker-bees. Carl Marx and Adam Smith, kind of ideological opposites, are on the same page on that part.

Invest: Adam Smith and Karl Marx.

We want our workers to be productive. We know almost all of them produce more when they use tools. Sometimes the most valuable tools are inside their heads, skills. Incredible productive leverage comes with a physical tool in the hands of the skilled worker. That's true for a worker very close to the bottom of the workforce hierarchy, and it's true at the top. Skilled workers give us more of the goods and services we want and need.

Skill is the payoff from investments in its development, training and practice. We benefit from investment in training, and a bigger investment usually produces a bigger payback. The kid who can operate a delivery truck is going to produce more value if he can also read the instructions, the address label on the package. Same is true farther up the skills ladder. The scholar just awarded a PhD in microbiology is more likely to develop useful understanding of the risk lurking in a newly discovered virus than would someone who barely made it through the course mandated for 10th graders in high school. The PhD represents a huge investment, probably another ten years beyond that first biology class.

Crucial as investment in people is, there's more. More investment, now, in the hardware and the software, in addition to training, will give the kids and grandkids a better shot at a future good life. And it's true we have more of what we want and need right now, partly thanks to good luck and certainly thanks to smart investments by our predecessors. They used science to gain understanding of their physical world, and they put some money to work to turn new understanding into new and better machines and finished products. They did so often knowing their investments would continue to pay dividends well beyond their own mortality. It wasn't all about just their own personal payback.

This is the other important piece to consider if you're trying to understand the ever-present balancing act, or tug of war, enjoying the good life on one end and the urge to be in, and real need to be in, the world of work at the other. Saving a handful of the grain, seeds for a future crop, or a slice of the bounty produced by hard work, maybe a little extra work, if *wisely* invested, will mean an even bigger bounty for the future good life.

Humans are like other living things in that we put away excess to make sure we survive when food to grab and eat immediately isn't available. We squirrel away. But we are unlike the other creatures in that we consciously invent new tools. And we put effort, some squirreled-away effort into that. We invest.

We squabble over "wisely." And there are always some humans who don't get the investing thing at all. A few, candidates for a Darwin Award, don't even get the idea that there will be hungry times if there's nothing in the larder. But those are the outliers. All of us here now are descendants of the smarter ones, the ones who saved so they wouldn't go hungry, and some who invested so that future good times would be better good times. Most agree there's merit to investing.

The very important qualifier is "wisely." In fact, putting that slice aside and "investing" it where it will just putrefy is stupid. An alternative, arguably a smarter one, is to simply eat it, make the feast a bigger fun-filled feast...now.

The question of what to do with the surplus has surely been a source of contention since day one. Through most of the human story the decision was made by the chief, or the chief and his close council. Or the king who simply said, "It's all mine, and I decide where to build the castle and who gets to eat and who doesn't." A quite simple answer.

We still have a few would-be kings, but they are mostly irrelevant. We're past that stage. It's more complicated now. Exactly who decides has become especially more unpredictable and complicated since we started using money. There's normally more of it than what is needed to transact business at the grocery store, so the question becomes what to do with the excess.

Investment is what we do wisely, or not, with the excess. Marx had a definite opinion on that. Don't give it to the capitalists.

The Speculators.

It's an identity not well regarded, skimmers who contribute nothing, some say. They just scoop a bit as the money flows by. They're not exactly thieves, though, maybe parasites a better noun. But that's not quite a fair indictment either, because we actually need speculators, risk takers.

And we are all speculators. Prediction is essential in the experience of life. Each of us wakes and speculates on what the day will bring and rarely is there not a bit of fog. We perceive reality through a fog of uncertainty. None of us can predict exactly how the day, or week, or year will end. We just have to make our best guess and proceed.

Investing is about that guess. The best of investors, including the ones who get it right for greatest return to the commonwealth, do so thanks to skill or luck at predicting the uncertain future. Their speculation produces good outcomes for the rest of us.

But there are speculators who care about nothing except their successful skim. They will move the money to any place it will enrich themselves, with no care whether it ultimately lands to seed a better future or it lands and putrefies. These speculators have no interest in building anything. They just play the market. Can we distinguish them from real investors who will build? We should, because it isn't just their skim that costs us. Our other loss is that as they move the money around, that money while it's simply being shuffled is not available for real constructive projects. Would-be genuinely beneficial ones are denied capital. Our surplus is misallocated, ironically or tragically, as some of the most outspoken advocates for Adam Smith capitalism shuffle the money to other places. It never becomes real capital. We suffer from underinvestment.

CHAPTER 5

SQUIRREL IT AWAY.

Reagonomics, etc.

"Greed is good," according to Gordon Gekko.[1] Ronald Reagan was accused of preaching the same thing. It was definitely an accusation when it came from folks who disagreed with Gekko.

Reaganomics was about tax cuts, especially big cuts for the folks who could most afford to pay taxes. The rationale was that because they were rich, they were obviously the smartest and the hardest working people. If we forced them to pay less to the government of each dollar they gained from competing to grab a piece of that big economic pie that is the American economy, they would work even harder, and their work would make the pie grow even bigger, faster. The underlying rationale for cutting taxes for the rich folks was that they had the money because they had earned it by delivering the goods. They were the smartest, hardest workers. Best to incentivize them.

The other important piece of the master plan was deregulation. The pitch was to "get the government off your back." Those pesky watchdogs, the federal cops, just got in the way of good work and innovation. They kept honest hard workers from producing all they could and would if they, especially the "entrepreneurial" ones, didn't have to worry about so many silly rules and regulations. It was a given that businesspeople are fundamentally honest, but if they should stray, the "market" will find them out and do the necessary disciplining. The other piece of the agenda was to chop away at huge wasteful spending of taxpayer money. No need to get very specific with the "wasteful" accusation. Everybody knows the government is huge, a huge bureaucracy, so the waste has to be huge. It was an appealing argument and Reagan's smiley style was perfect for delivering it; with the government out of your pocket and off your back...prosperity and freedom!

In the 1980s an out of the mainstream (crackpot in the opinion of some) economist, Arthur Laffer, influenced the Reagan supply-side approach to policy. The "Laffer Curve"[2] illustrated so easily and clearly that tax rates could be too high. His curve showed that government revenues could go down if rates were increased. People would quit paying taxes because they'd quit working if the government tried to take too much. Logically to keep the government adequately funded, best to have a lower the tax rate.

Laffer has since receded even further out of sight and mind, and early claims of Reaganomics success have been written down. A contemporary voice, about as out of the mainstream as Laffer is Peter Navaro, [3] a sometimes-important Trump whisperer. He doesn't focus on taxes so much; sort of says not to worry because tariffs will take care of everything.

The record.

The country's economic performance since Eisenhower (1953-1961) has been a little better during Democratic administrations than Republican ones. Reagan had pretty good numbers, average growth rate 3.5%, a little better than his predecessor Carter at 3.3% but not as good as Democrat Clinton at 3.9%. Later Bush and Trump presidencies had rather mediocre economic performance, too. There just isn't much evidence that the promised benefits from lightening the tax burden on the wealthy (Republican Orthodoxy) have materialized.

What has materialized is significantly greater inequality in the distribution of the country's wealth. The top 1% claimed 27% in 2025, the bottom half of households less than 6%.[4]

Of course, there certainly was inequality before Reagan. In 1989, before the policy effects became significant, Federal Reserve data show the top 1% had about 20%, the lower half around 7%.[5]

There is room for debate over how wide the gap (precision) between rich and poor has become, but there's no debate that it is wide, dangerously so in the opinion of many students of economic and political history. There is also no disagreement that a large cohort of Americans feel they are struggling to survive. They aren't getting enough of the pie, and they also know that those at the top have more than they can possibly eat.

Gekko plan total nonsense?

Clearly there is evidence the Gordon Gekko economic plan hasn't produced the benefits it promised. Could it be the premise is just plain wrong? Is looking out for number one totally nonsense? Absolutely not. Nobody survives unless they look out for number one, take some for themselves. Complete self-denial is suicide. Every living thing is the progeny of some previous living thing that acted selfishly when it had to.

Gordon used the word greed. A logical extension of his advocacy is that greedy people are good people. By the same logic, if you're not greedy, you're not a good person? Or could it be if not greedy, maybe you're just not normal? Or maybe a phony, a fake.

According to Webster greed is: "A selfish and excessive desire for more of something (such as money) than is needed." Webster is the authority on what the word means. To get the whole thing though, you have to read the whole thing. Hmm. "...more than is needed."

Squirrels hide nuts. Bees make honey and guard it. If you doubt the guarding part, stick your hand into a hive to grab a scoop of that precious stuff. Bees think it's theirs, their property, not for sharing.

Dogs bury bones, and people squirrel away, too. We all sometimes have more than we need, and we hold onto the excess, at least some of it…instead of share. Are we all greedy?

Okay, we store surplus because we know how quickly surplus can turn into not enough. It's the experience of every living thing, even very simple life forms, like algae cells in stagnant pond water, for example. They survive the night on excess energy captured from sunlight in the middle of the day. Their middle of the day more-than-enough is squirreled away.

Closer relatives do the same thing. Bears, fat at the end of summer, stay alive as they sleep through the winter and eat nothing. People get fat, too, some just not knowing when they've squirreled away enough.

Storing is about survival, to make it through the night, or the winter when there aren't berries in the woods. There are scarce times. For humans there always have been. And there always have been at least some survivors. You and I wouldn't be here if every one of our ancestors hadn't made it through the famine and the drought. Obviously, prudence with the extra was good. Having enough in the larder to get through is damn important. Surviving is good.

Back to Webster. "More...than is needed." Could it be here is the problem, why we even have the word in our dictionary? The question is: How much is more? And is there wiggle room, some space for a judgement call? Maybe we'd agree greedy is the proper adjective when it's way more than enough. Important from Webster are two additional words, "excessive desire." Incidentally, Gordon Gekko certainly wasn't the first to observe and offer an opinion. In the words of a fictional character in a tale about money, love, and flood, Shot At and Missed...And Florida Goin' Under, old Ben Childress, in his nineties, but with his wits mostly intact, put it this way, "The greediest sons-a-bitches want it all."

---

[1] Michael Douglas won an Academy Award playing this character in the movie "Wall Street." He was a scoundrel, a pretend composite of some real scoundrels, like Ivan Boesky and Michael Milken. They and others were the thieves of the 1980s, some of them probably emboldened by Ronald Reagan's promise to "get the government off your back."

[2] https://americanhistory.si.edu/collections/object/nmah_1439217

[3] https://www.newyorker.com/magazine/2025/12/29/peter-navarro-profile

[4] https://fred.stlouisfed.org/release/tables?rid=453&eid=813804&od=

[5] Precision with these numbers is a bit of an illusion. Exactly how much the really wealthy can claim as "theirs" is an estimate and also subject to the whims of financial markets. One resource estimated 31% as the value held by the top 1% of households, and the bottom half of households claiming a meager 2.5% of the whole. https://inequality.org/article/billionaire-wealth-concentration-is-even-worse-than-you-imagine/

CHAPTER 6

ORIGINAL WELFARE.

Caring.

At the opposite end, away from Gekko, there is another behavior older than the species. We help when somebody stumbles. Sick or injured and can't hunt or forage, we bring them food and maybe drag them to shelter. It's just what we do and have been doing for a very long time.

There's survival logic to it. Instead of fangs and claws, we evolved with an oversized brain that allowed us to collaborate for safety and sustenance. We banded together, and the size of the band mattered. If it got too big, collaboration would devolve into chaos because the leader, who had that role probably because he or she had natural traits that were good for keeping the band, or tribe, on task toward meeting some important survival need, would run out of bandwidth. If there were too many humans, each with a brain and the urge for some agency of their own, the chief would just lose control. Too many and it wouldn't hold together.

But not enough could mean disaster, too. If too few members, death to those remaining, at the hands of a neighboring band or hungry neighbors of a different species, was likely. Survival depended on keeping the numbers up. The tribes that survived, our ancestors, did so by keeping their number up, and important to that success was the habit of helping the other recover when he or she fell or was struggling for a bit with injury or illness. Humans cared for other adults just like they cared for their immature offspring. They cared for each other. This was original welfare. As hunter-gatherers settled into villages, original welfare settled in, too. It was and is, evolved behavior for survival, not something ordered from above through a monk or magician standing on a mountaintop, who then inscribed it onto a tablet that humans obey because it is inscribed. Caring for each other is just what we do. Failing to care is a deviation from the norm.

There is inherent conflict, though. It's back to the old "looking out for number one" mandate. You can't completely count on somebody else showing up when you're in need. Kids get it, pretty early on, that momma won't always be there. They figure it out that when you're hungry you grab the morsel quickly before the other kid gets it. Some do need a little more coaching on the idea of sharing. Coaching is where the tablet comes in. There is a message. Most kids live with it at home so only need an occasional reminder. For all, it's repeated at school. "Be nice to your fellow human."

Outliers.

The surviving tribes—that's us—got the message, the one on the tablet. And we tell ourselves, in our stories, that the message is who we are, what we do. But there are outliers, including some awful ones. Throughout history there have been psychopathic killers. Hitler and Stalin and Pol Pot[1] presided over genocides. They are condemned because they were apparently happy to murder millions and impose suffering on millions more. Others, perhaps thousands, are not as recognized because their atrocities were on a much smaller scale. Some of those most senior evil participants in Hitler's rampage defended themselves at the Nuremburg Trials [2] by saying they were simply "following orders." Some of them managed to escape justice for decades by running to obscure places in South America and blending in.

These awful examples of human behavior are extreme. They are outliers way beyond normal for our species. We are vigilant to recognize and thwart any who would repeat in the future. But there are other outliers.

Not nice, but not sociopaths.

Way short of pure evil, another group of not quite normal-for-the-species humans needs our consideration, too, the ones who for some reason were never exposed to the message on the tablet, or who read it and thought it just another clever con by some hungry and dangerous survivor like themselves. They see the world as a two-year old. "Mine, mine, mine!" they say. Old Ben Childress had it right. "The greediest sons-a-bitches want it all."

But maybe it's not quite so clear cut. Human behaviors don't quantify with digital precision. It's not either "on" or "off" but more often, sort of on or off, sometimes, or somewhat. Most people are sort of greedy or sort of generous and often a bit grumpy. Some are greedier but not miserly to the point of total disregard for any other person's survival.

The gray band between saintly and dark evil is wide. And that presents a major challenge. In order for those among us who fall injured or sick to not suffer additional misery, we must give them a hand. Resources must be handed to them, and sometimes it must be pulled in the direction that would be the natural choice of the saints, the direction that would be normal for those most generous. It means diverting a slice from those with plenty. How big a slice becomes an immediate point of contention, partly because that slice has to pay for other important things as well, like roads, bridges, and education. Sometimes agency and resources must be yanked back from the greediest. They are forced to share some of their hoard.

There's more to it than that, of course, the certainty of taxes. The survival imperative to "squirrel some away" is in all of us. And we proclaim quite explicitly, "This is mine." We live together with rules that include the right to do exactly that. We honor claims of property. We protect claims of property. We have standards for what is fair, and that includes for treatment of each other as fellow human beings and for treatment of our property claims.

Caring for our fellows who are struggling to care for themselves is fundamental human behavior. Societies have long cared collectively for their members who are struggling, and often have done it through the church, the appeal being kindness for the poor in this world will be rewarded in the next. When kindness falls short, taxes fill the gap.

Just like in an ancient world, we still have the poor, and we help them. But other parts of our modern world, what we experience, are very different from those of our predecessors of millennia or hundreds of millennia past. Much of our vista is of our own construction, and it serves us because its interdependencies are constructive. They work because they are tied together with infrastructure, much of it requiring investment on a scale that no private property holder would be willing or able to make on their own. Even an Elon Musk could not build the Interstate Highway System. These essential elements of a modern society are collectively funded and owned productive assets. They are made possible through the collection of some of the excess that we as individuals would otherwise squirrel away. They are paid for with taxes, which can only come from those who have the money. That includes especially those with a lot of money.

---

[1] In the late 1970s as much as a fourth of the population of Cambodia's almost 8 million was killed by the Khmer Rouge at the direction of the Pol Pot regime. https://en.wikipedia.org/wiki/Cambodian_genocide

[2] Herman Goering was Hitler's second in command. This story of his trial at Nuremberg is captured in the movie "Nuremberg" starring Russell Crowe. https://www.bbc.com/culture/article/20251023-a-forgotten-chapter-in-the-history-of-the-nuremberg-trials

CHAPTER 7

SMARTEST IN THE ROOM.

Superstars.

There probably was a time when you were the smartest guy in the room. It could have been third grade. Your hold on the title likely was brief, maybe until you missed a couple words on a spelling quiz. Or it could be you got bumped when another kid's retired school-teacher grandmother moved in at his house and started tutoring.

Somebody's at the top at the end of 5th grade. The younger kids might think he or she, the one at the top, is the smartest in the whole school.

But then comes middle school. Three elementary schools send three smartest kids. And then high school for the kids from two middle schools. Now there's six smartest kids, and that's just in the 9th grade. There's a bunch of smarties in each of the other three grades, too.

There might be 1200 students in that school, and some are close to brilliant. Just one finishes at the top, each year, Valedictorian. She can probably go next to any college or university she wants.

Smartest in the room.

It could be getting far away is her plan, and Stanford says yes. Off from Maine she goes, all the way to California. Could be the other way, Bowdoin College in Brunswick, Maine, away from brutal-desert Phoenix. Probably not a complete shock, but sobering anyway, the new freshman discovers the place is crawling with valedictorians, all these smartest guys in the room!

Most of us come to the realization that nobody is the smartest. One exception would be when there's just one. If you're solo, take pleasure in knowing that at the moment there's nobody smarter than you in your little closet.

It's an annual ritual, smart kids going off on the first step to fame and fortune based on smarts. Some keep at it and get the degree. Some keep getting smarter and getting more degrees. Some quit and go make money instead. Gates quit Harvard. So did Zuckerberg. Musk quit a PhD program at Stanford, but he'd already earned a bachelor's in physics and another one in economics. Bezos managed only one, but it is an impressive credential, magna cum laude in Electrical Engineering and Computer Science, from Princeton. Mark Zuckerberg and Bill Gates didn't even get very far along on the bachelor's degree at Harvard.

Dropouts with the money.

The four above are all fantastically rich. There are no PhDs and each has more than $100 billion. It's doubtful many of the brightest kids who went on to the Doctor of Something recognition have $100 million, or $10 million. Remember ten billion is a thousand times as much as ten million.

The disparity in measurable compensation (accumulation) is striking. The PhD in microbiology represents eight or ten years of study. Hard work. And if it's you as the degree candidate, while you do that hard work you will likely have to borrow some money just to make your rent and eat. You'll have to pay it back when you start getting a paycheck. If your field is science or engineering, or if you earn an MD instead of PhD, you'll be able to pay off your loans and live fairly comfortably. You can plan a vacation once in a while, and you'll be able to help your own kids with the cost of their education. You might even sometimes fly first class. You won't own your own jet or ship, though, or an island in the Caribbean. In contrast, the billionaires who dropped out of school can have any or all of it.

Everybody goes to school. We all know school is work, your job when you're a kid. We all know it's hard, sometimes even if you're really smart. Hardly anybody thinks a PhD is a simple thing that anybody, especially the dumbest guy in the class can have handed to them. To earn a PhD you have to work, and you have to be quite smart. The billionaires don't have PhDs.

But are they smart? It's a pretty good bet they are. First off, nobody, like the ones mentioned above, gets into an Ivy League school (Harvard, Princeton) or a PhD program at Stanford unless an admissions officer or committee sees real promise, a kid in front of them with some serious brain power. Most of the others on the billionaires list didn't land there by winning the lottery, or stupidity that turned out lucky. Exceptions may be a few of second or third generation who were born with a silver spoon in their mouth. They are the aberrations among the aberrantly rich. Most of the billionaires are smart. So what?

Smartest in the room.

Whose opinion should count?

Well, how about the question of whether to give more weight to the opinion of the smart ones among us rather than those closer to the other end of the brainy scale. We could take advice about an approaching asteroid from a PhD astrophysicist more seriously than that from an old lady with a funny hat and a broomstick who has her own YouTube channel. We might pay more attention when a billionaire talks about money than the guy coming out of a convenience store with $20 of lottery tickets mumbling and grumbling about not winning a jackpot yet.

The thing is, we might be smart to let smart people make some of the big decisions, ones that affect all of us. It would be smart to let the smart ones be the leaders. Maybe the smartest ones should make most of the decisions, or all the decisions. If we changed our thinking about the possibility that there could be "the smartest" person, then it would make sense to let that person make all the decisions. Not workable, of course.

There are two tracks here. By smart we usually mean knowing stuff, and knowing how to use what you know, your tricks of the trade. Logically, the more work you've put into gathering knowledge and tricks the smarter you would be. If you've been a scholar for 20 years, you're probably smarter than the newbie with only 2 years of study. You would probably be the one recognized as an expert. We do take advice from experts.

The other track is more direct-evidence based, as in dollars you can count. The guy with a huge pile of money is obviously smart. Almost all of the money guys are smart, including some who are thieves and have the money because they stole it. They usually, but not always, stay out of jail. We don't generally recognize them as experts, but we sure do consider their opinions on the really big decisions.

CHAPTER 8

THE MATH PROBLEM.

How much?

Kids who love math…adults too, are a minority. Math is hard. The fact that it's hard, and most of us shy away when possible is a gift for some. Opportunists do the math and then get more money out of our pockets because *we* don't.

But good people do good math, too. In addition to answering the question, "what's for lunch?" somebody does the math on "how many" for lunch. And then somebody better do some more math to figure out how much is needed for that many.

There are important numbers all around us. You would certainly hope the architect or engineer did the math right when designing the roof over your head or the brakes on your car. It is math to design and make stuff and use stuff efficiently. We need numbers.

Big number. Really big number.

There is a problem, though. We sometimes don't see the difference between a big number and a really big number, or a tiny amount and a really tiny amount, like a nanogram. We don't get it, what a billion is. We don't figure out that a billionaire really is extraordinary compared to a millionaire. A billionaire is unusual. Some people who do the math are rightly in awe[1] of billionaires.

An order of magnitude is another way to think about it. An order of magnitude means ten times as much. Consider this grocery store example: Ten grapes would take up about the same amount of space as a mandarin orange. The orange is an order of magnitude larger than a grape. Ten oranges or a hundred grapes, two orders of magnitude and a bagful at the grocery store. Ten bags, a thousand grapes, three orders of magnitude. That's the millionaire compared to you, the thousandaire. Bump it up another three orders and it's a truckload. Bezos, Musk, Ellison, Zuckerberg, et. al. each have hundreds of truckloads, and you have one grape. You're supposed to survive on one grape. You have one and the entry-level billionaire has a thousand million. You're hungry, thinking about what else you might scrounge to survive, and the hundreds-of-billions-billionaire is thinking wine, and locked cellars to squirrel away from you his thousands, or tens of thousands, of *cases* of grape juice.

It's our nature to calculate, to estimate, and we do often get it wrong. But pretty early on, even kids get it right that a $10 bill is better than a $1 bill. It will get you three cones with three scoops of ice cream in each, a much larger treat than one scoop. And pretty early on, they also learn that for a buck you probably can't even get a cone with nothing in it. We do math. We quantify and qualify.

It quickly can get confusing though, when it's ten times something and then ten times that and ten times that. An order of magnitude difference means one number is ten times as large as the other. If I have $20 and you have $200, you have an order of magnitude more money than me. Mary with $2,000 has an order of magnitude more than you and two orders more than me. Barbie with $20,000 puts her an order of magnitude above Mary. Pauper me has a $20 bill for breakfast, lunch and dinner. You have a wad that will fit in your pocket, and Mary has a hundred of them, enough to slightly bulge her fanny pack. This Barbie would have a ten fanny packs.

But the real Mary Millionaire ($2 million) has a thousand times as much as the Mary above, a thousand fanny packs. And the real Barbie has a thousand times that, a million fanny packs. You have ten bills, and I have one measly strip with Andrew Jackson's image on it.

Mary and Barbie.

Unfortunately, some of the honest folks who do the math, including the math for what it takes to put groceries on the table and a roof over your head, have unintentionally muddied the waters even as they try to wake us from our weak-math fog about governance and fairness. Bernie Sanders, demanding a fairer deal for everybody who is not in that exclusive club of aberrants at the top, sometimes links millionaires and billionaires in the same sentence. It sounds like a billionaire is not much different, maybe just a little bit richer than a millionaire. But it's not a little difference, one of them having just somewhat more money. Barbie Billionaire has a thousand times as much, three orders of magnitude more than Mary Millionaire. Mary doesn't have 1%. She has one-tenth of 1% as much as Barbie. She's in abject poverty by comparison.

Truth is, Mary is doing okay and is better off than most folks, the worker-bees making $25 an hour, for example. She's doing very much better than the single-paycheck ones with kiddies who want to eat and have shoes to wear. That twenty-five-dollar worker wage gets you $52,000 in a year. Mary on the other hand, if she earns just an average investment return (S&P 500) on her one mil, and doesn't bring in anything else, like from a job, will have $70,000 to spend. She can eat without having to eat any of her nest egg.

How about Barbie? Poor Barbie has to struggle to get by with a thousand times as much, $70,000,000 a year. But she might pay more tax. Without a good financial planner or clever accountant, it might be a check to the government for $20,000,000. Of course it's highly unlikely she wouldn't have an advisor. Just a tiny piece of that tax bill, if avoided, would be an okay paycheck for a "tax planning" professional. It is inconceivable that she hasn't had offers of help. But if Barbie was naïve or just didn't care, and paid the full amount, she'd have to buy groceries and cover the rent with the $4,000,000 a month left over. Not "poor" Barbie.

Ahh…the tax man. Mary gets hit, too, but not as hard as Barbie, maybe pays 20%. She'll have 56K left for rent and groceries, a little more than a thousand a week.

Worker-bee pays taxes too. It's likely 15% counting sales taxes and contributions to Social Security and Medicare trust funds. There could even be some income taxes owed. The worker-bee $52,000 shrinks to $44,200. It's $850 a week, and the car needs an oil change, the kids have a dental appointment, and eggs are still $8 a dozen...and the rent.

Of course, some are getting a better deal. It's not a completely black and white situation, all the well-off being really well off and all the workers impoverished. Some worker-bees make way more than $25 and do just fine. And for Mary, a million in the bank is good, but it's no guarantee. If she has no expectation of getting more money, she'd best be prudent. Get a bad break or get sick or simply live too long and her million might not even be enough.

But Barbie has plenty. She can vacation for 12 months of the year. She could even buy her own jet and hire a couple pilots to fly her anywhere she wants to go for vacation. She could buy a politician or two, or maybe a hundred of them. You might say she has *more* than she needs.

Envy her, we might, but let's not be too critical. Could be she's a nice person, and maybe she didn't steal her pile of money. Could be she's been rewarded for creating something really valuable for the rest of us.

However she got her money, she is extraordinarily rich. She has way more than she needs. And a fact to consider, even lower-level worker-bee probably *occasionally* has more than he or she needs. Mary usually has more than enough but occasionally not, or it at least feels like not enough. Barbie always has more than enough.

---

[1] Awe: "emotion variously combining dread, veneration, and wonder…" according to Webster.

CHAPTER 9

MONEY CONSCIOUS TIPPING POINT.

Flamboyant Money.

The question hit a consciousness level tipping point for some of us when Jeff Bezos or Elon Musk or one of the less flamboyant of the money superstars hit $200 billion of personal wealth. An exact date isn't important, but the timeframe is.

Donald Trump was on the scene, the President, proudly marketing his gold-plated brand to a new, wider audience. The pitch was: Wealth is virtue. Trump convinced his MAGA followers that they were all in the same tent, with him in the virtuous club. Happy days were here again. The scolds who kept harping on economic and social disparities and slightly more theoretical stuff and scientific stuff, like climate change, were on the run. America was going to be great again.

COVID-19.

But then the pandemic upset everything. The President himself was enfeebled for several days as the virus took over his body. COVID probably cost him reelection in 2020. There was a significant economic impact, on the downside, and Trump was a convenient target for some of the blame.

Despite his trying to make it a non-event and claiming a bleach treatment would make it go away, the rest of the world knew better. People got sick and many died. Avoiding exposure was the only available strategy because most knew the president's snake oil suggestion was nonsense, and there wasn't yet a vaccine or effective treatment. Worldwide, people stopped traveling, even to work or to the grocery store, unless absolutely necessary. They stopped burning oil to go places.

It was probably a consciousness tipping point for the president, though he never admitted it. It had to have felt like freefall. Surely it was a "holy crap" moment in the oil patch, too, with demand falling off a cliff. All the world's tanker ships quickly filled and then steamed a mile offshore and anchored. A measure of the level of panic was the plummet of oil futures prices to well below zero. If you held a contract for oil delivery from a US producer (WTI – West Texas Intermediate crude oil) previously worth $70 or $80 a barrel, you owned those barrels, and you were stuck, because nobody wanted any more oil. At one point it was worthless, and $37/barrel was what you would have to pay somebody to haul it away. WTI sold for minus $37. Not the root cause of the crash to negative but maybe the trigger, the shove over the precipice, was the spat between Russia and Saudi Arabia. Negotiators couldn't agree on who would cut production and how much.

The crude cartoon version of the scene was of a couple angry guys across the table from each other, one, probably the Russian, pounding his fist, then standing and yelling, “Fuck you!” The response was, “No, fuck you!” The Saudis cut prices and cranked up the pumps. Oil crashed.

There was a cool off and then an agreement to collaborate on supply and avoid the disaster of lasting price collapse, recognition that a temporary squeeze on the cash flow was way better than no cash flow. No doubt there was a blink. Putin survived and the Saudi’s knew they would be better off long term with a big piece of the market at $60 a barrel rather than the whole thing at $20...and being the target of attack and sabotage from every quarter.

Happy campers...not.

Another impact of the pandemic probably not anticipated was attention drawn to a festering political problem that both parties much prefer to avoid if possible. Financial stress long suffered by people in the bottom half of the country’s economy especially, came into focus because COVID-19 was the story of the day, and personal accounts always add interest. The personal grabs attention, so there’s promise of a bigger payoff to those who earn a living telling the story of the day. Partly because of a decades-long migration of wealth into the hands of those at the top and away from everybody else, half the population has a stress story to tell.

Trump got pushed out, and a new crew, with President Joe Biden at the top and a majority in Congress, came to town and pushed through emergency measures that kept the health crisis from also becoming an economic crisis. People got emergency checks from the government, and they continued to buy their groceries and pay the rent.

The pandemic receded, thanks to an effective vaccine, and the economy recovered. But people weren't happy. The 2024 election results made that obvious. Perhaps perception, not necessarily reality, is what counted. For sure, there is also still quite a fascination with Trump gold.

The Republicans came back and immediately cut taxes, sending a lot more of the money right to the top. The returned Republican President started plastering the White House with gilt. He tore down a third of it to build a new grand ballroom, no doubt envisioned to be a golden display case for The Era of Trump.

A year into the second Trump term, the people again weren't exactly happy. In addition to some outright nastiness, insults, appointments to important positions of individuals with less than stellar qualifications, and high impact acts of retribution, an elephant in the room is the perception that the economy still isn't great. Even though the unemployment numbers are okay, jobs don't feel plentiful, and groceries and rent are still high.

In addition to the reasons for grumpiness above, the visuals haven't been flattering. The inauguration stage put names and faces on the billionaires who are hoarding the money. Then Trump's decision to put Elon Musk up on a bulldozer and tell him to plow it through any place in Washington he wants to, was probably a dumb mistake. Musk, jumping up and down, chainsaw in hand, wasn't quite what the American people thought they'd signed on for.

DOGE[1] was a clown performance, entertaining at first. But then there were unintended consequences, like a sudden bright light awareness that "they" really did want to come after Social Security. And there was a new awareness of billionaires. "Who is that guy?" Maybe noticed for the first time...and he's worth how much? And really that crazy? Cybertruck? And he says he's going after Social Security next! "Whoa!"

Musk wasn't on the stage for long, even though his show can be pretty exciting. And give him credit, he is a sometimes visionary. Space X and Tesla are not trivial accomplishments, and he has certainly been a factor in those successes. But his act doesn't play well with all audiences. EVs are not a natural fit with MAGA, and he sometimes seems almost suicidal with comments that can be interpreted as echoes of Nazi thought from 80 years ago. A slew of Tesla drivers apologetically point out that they bought their cars well before Elon revealed himself.

The show (DOGE) pretty quickly grew stale, maybe because it quickly became obvious that people valued government services and financial support and some of those were subject to the axe or club. The other thing was, it seemed Musk was capturing more of the headlines than his boss. Could be there wasn't enough room on the stage.

The other explanation is that maybe there was a realization it was time to get back to the main project, the money, the real money. The DOGE adventure and bad press hit the Tesla stock price. Loss for Elon at one point could very well have been over $100 billion. Christmas eve, 2024 the price hit $462/share. By early spring it was bouncing along at about $230/share. Investors weren't happy. The ones who stuck it out, though, felt much better by the end of the year. The December 24, 2025 price was back up to $485/share, and that same week the Delaware Supreme Court restored Musk's contested $139 billion pay package from 2018,[2] bumping his net worth now to above $700 billion. The trillion-dollar mark doesn't look out of reach.

Let that sink in for a moment, another order (actually three orders) of magnitude phenomenon. A trillionaire would have a thousand times as much as a billionaire who has a thousand times as much as a millionaire who has a thousand times as much as you if you have a thousand one-dollar bills. And let this sink in. If that's all *you* have, you're not really special. Some estimates are that 13 million American households have negative net worth, less than zero in the pocket.[3]

The tipping point question. Why?

It's actually two questions. Why do so many people have less than nothing? That one is complicated. There might be 13 million reasons, or at least 13 million contributing factors. It also could be there are a couple factors common to all those 13 million stories. But the other question, why billionaires? Why do they have so much money? Why do we have billionaires?

Could it be because we have decided we should, that there should be billionaires? Have we decided that somebody can have $100 billion, or $700 billion. Have we decided that Elon Musk can soon claim a trillion dollars as his? If he can get his hands on it, should he be able to keep **ALL** the money?

Not long ago, asking questions with those kinds of numbers would have you laughed out of the room. $100 billion is a ridiculously large number. But it isn't. Now every one of the wealthiest twenty individuals likely top it,[4] with a half dozen passing the $200 billion mark. The questioning is starting to show up where you wouldn't normally expect it, like even in the Wall Street Journal.

---

[1] DOGE Department of Government Efficiency was a creation of the new Trump Administration. Musk claimed there was a couple trillion dollars of taxpayer savings just waiting for someone to break open the jar and liberate it. The jar, of course, was the government bureaucracy. Trump handed Elon the sledgehammer.

[2] https://www.cnn.com/2025/12/19/business/musk-pay-package-latest

---

[3] https://finance.yahoo.com/news/13-million-american-households-negative-160705078.html

[4] Mid-summer 2025 the club had eighteen but approaching the end of the year the stock market was on a tear. No doubt a few names have been added to the list. https://www.businessinsider.com/wealth-billionaires-musk-bezos-zuckerberg-net-worth-jensen-huang-waltoans-2024-8

CHAPTER 10

SO WHAT?

Fairness.

We have people with extraordinary wealth, more than most Americans by many orders of magnitude. Why does it matter?

It matters on several counts. The first is the notion of simple fairness. We expect a fair deal whenever and with whomever we deal. We trade money for a product or service, and we receive money for anything we sell. We expect to get what we pay for and normally have to pay for what we get. We pay taxes and receive back a share of public goods, use of public infrastructure for transportation, for example. We receive benefit from the efforts of a publicly trained, in tax-funded-schools, workforce. We receive the benefit of a publicly funded court system and enforcement of laws created to hold the roughest and most selfish, the bullies and thieves, in check. We are protected by our military against organized bullies and thieves from outside our borders.

Our public benefit is more or less proportional to our contribution. That is the fairness rationale for progressive taxation. It is recognition of the fact that if your payoff from the shared economy is larger, very likely it is because you work in collaboration with a workforce made more valuable to you because of public investment in education, your product is delivered over public infrastructure, and because you have wealth that would surely be the target of thieves, you receive greater benefit from police, the courts, and the nation's military. Your income and wealth are proportional to the public benefit you have received. Fairness would dictate that billionaires pay taxes proportional to their benefit, like everyone else.

Fairness is important for two reasons. Quality of life, especially the sense that as humans we all have a shot at the pleasant moments as well as risk of suffering the nasty ones. We are beneficiaries and victims of chance. Life is good if we're all in this scramble playing by the same rules and equally subject to the whims of fate.

Secondly, and damaging beyond the immediate, is the negative effect a sense of unfairness can have on the synergy benefits possible when we collaborate. The perception of unfairness discourages joint effort, and without that we are much less productive. United we stand. Divided we fall. United we produce. If it's unfair, we have the very logical urge to just say, "eh...why bother?"

America called itself the "land of opportunity." The Statue of Liberty was the welcoming symbol. Lady Liberty beckoned, and immigrants, energetic, optimistic, and often frustrated by the world they left behind, came and worked and melded. It is a success story. It is a multi-generation success story. Children of immigrants grew up with the idea of reward for work, and they embraced their home and enjoyed its bounty, and they became leaders. Their experience was mostly fair, and their perception was that it was fair. Their children assumed it was a fair deal, and they worked and produced. Surely continuation of the success story is more likely if the belief continues. The next generation must believe the competition is fair. The next wave of hopeful and energetic immigrants must see the United States as a place of fairness.

Investment: Not enough where needed.

The ultra-wealthy are not hungry. Adam Smith's entrepreneur was a hungry worker and an investor in the purest sense. He was a forward thinker, confident that his efforts to use his wits and every tool in his kit would be rewarded by the market. Protecting his cache was an impulse secondary to his drive to honestly compete to increase that cache. In comparison, the modern ultra-wealthy are more risk averse. Holding on to the hoard is their first impulse. As they hold, investments with high returns, particularly those with high returns that flow to the public generally and aren't easily captured by individuals, are delayed because sufficient funds just aren't available.

This is particularly true if time risk is a major factor. The payoff for fundamental research in biology or medicine, for example, can be decades in the future, and the same is clearly true for climate protection investment. In the case of climate, the time horizon is immediate out though centuries into the future. Billionaires don't put their billions to work on this very high potential but distant-return investment unless forced to.

Now, a fourth of the way into the 21st century, the economy can thrive only if real capital investments are made wisely. Wise now, what is needed now, is quite different from what was needed by the private sector and public sector a hundred years ago or what was needed in the mid-twentieth century. In 1950 coal mines were essential, air travel except for military purposes was exotic and viewed as a somewhat risky luxury good, not essential to commerce and normal family ties, as it is now. Investment in building air travel infrastructure was not as important.

In 1950, education beyond high school, except for veterans under the GI Bill,[1] was available and wanted by a minority reaching workforce age. A fourth of the girls in high school learned the typewriter. All girls took "home economics," and all the boys had at least a year of "shop class." Some girls learned to drive a car. Twelve years of schooling was enough.

People then had a radio at home and most knew the term electronics had something to do with it. If the radio died, a repair shop could usually bring it back to life by replacing a burned-out tube. That simple AM receiver had maybe a half dozen vacuum tubes. *If you've never seen one, they're kind of like an incandescent light bulb about the size and shape of a small cucumber or zucchini.*

In 1947 nobody had even heard of a transistor, because it hadn't been invented yet. Most did know that the military was messing with electronics, all kinds of stuff that wasn't made of wood or produced in a steel mill and didn't grow on the farm, things like radar and atomic bombs. Guys who went into the service got more training.

The first transistor, invented in 1947 could do the same thing a vacuum tube did, change a stream of electrons. In comparison it was tiny.

Soon there were transistor radios, some that would fit in the palm of your hand. Then came circuit boards with dozens or hundreds of transistors and then printed circuits with soldered on "chips" and motherboards, computers.

Moore's Law, and Steven Jobs and company, gave us the iPhone. New ones today have maybe 20 billion transistors doing calculations measured in gigaflops, or teraflops (trillion floating-point operations per second), way more than the biggest mainframe machine IBM could offer in 1970 or maybe even more than any available at the turn of the millennium.

Folks who graduated high school in 1950, prepared for work then, but who never went back, would be useless if plopped down in front of a control panel for a crew of robots or an assembly line, today. Then it was an analog world of physical work. Bend, lift, carry...or hand shovel, and controlling a machine meant moving a handle left or right, front or back, or maybe rotating a valve to shut off or slightly change some liquid flow. Half those grads in 1950 had probably yet to see a television screen for the first time. Twelve years of school was maybe enough.

Now work world is on a screen or multiple screens. Multiple giant ones on the far wall with the worker at his desk, his clone at the next desk, and the next, obviously on task with multiple smaller screens close in front of him or her is the paradigm image of today. The facial expression is one of seriousness and professional competence.

Not explicit in the image is the fact that professional competence is likely built on advanced specialized knowledge, knowledge only gained through an extended period of study. Professional competence, knowledge-skill competence, is the essential ingredient now for economic productivity, not human muscle. Robots do the lifting. Humans tell the robots what and where to lift. Going forward, artificial intelligence will assume more and more control of the bots, and humans will control the AI. At least that is the prediction of our less pessimistic visionaries.

Skilled workers today need understanding of energy, engineering, math, biology, and economics. And their work might produce greater payback to the larger neighborhood if they have a better understanding of politics, that device that always interacts with the economic consequences of their good work. Workers need communication skills, including knowledge of the communications hardware and software. They must also be able to communicate in specialized communications terms. They work collaboratively so must communicate with other humans in addition to the machines.

Consensus on need at the beginning of the 20th century resulted in the adoption of 12 years of schooling as standard. Investment in raising everyone's level of knowledge was seen as wise use of the money. Universal public education became the norm worldwide.

Toward the end of the millennium, however, evidence grew that a 12-year investment is not enough. And parts of the curriculum thought normal and essential to nurture a child from wild and unproductive ward at age 6, into productive adult at age 18, have been sacrificed. Music and art, and industrial arts and home economics, and even physical education have been curtailed to make room for emphasis on what we now call STEM, science, technology, engineering and math.

Civics, that knowledge exercise to learn the rules, how to live as citizens in a free society, has mostly disappeared from the course list. There just isn't enough time.

Sacrifice of time for instruction to appreciate the refined expressions of human experience, art, and diverting that time to the practical arts of the day leads to lost opportunity to enjoy completely the fruits of practical arts advancement. Evidence of loss is a public discourse that is now cruder, with more shouting and posturing, and deception is closer to the acceptable norm. We lose because having to examine every incoming message for danger and lies is not a quality-of-life enhancement.

In the simplest of terms, we need to invest more in education. The standard should be increased to maybe sixteen years, and those years might or might not necessarily involve a credential as formally defined as a college degree.

We live in a time when knowledge, not bricks and mortar, or land, or minerals below the surface, are the most valuable assets. In fact, we may be approaching the time when extraction at large scale is no longer needed. We can reemploy and reshape our bricks and mortar to meet the needs of our knowledge economy and the realities of climate change. Soon it may be that knowledge is the only significantly high-value, and in fact irreplaceable, asset.

As was recognized at the start of the twentieth century, the private sector would not or could not step up and provide funding for twelve years of learning. There was agreement for public education paid for with public funds, taxes. It's likely our needed money source is no different today. A slice of extraordinarily accumulating wealth can and should be invested now to assure availability for all, sixteen years of formal education.

Lazy or scared? Passive.

With exceptions, wealthy people, like everybody else, get lazy. And they become more risk averse. Investment involves risk, but the money doesn't work unless it is invested. If Elon had all the money, and he decided to just stand guard beside the pile and not let any of it go to work, we would all be the losers.

That is not a particularly good hypothetical, however, at least in part because he is in many ways an outlier, a bit of a crazy man and sometimes risk taker, not a truly representative billionaire. But the scenario, with perhaps some other extreme wealth hoarder standing guard, is plausible.

Economists, especially those who consider themselves monetarists, track a variable called money velocity. The Federal Reserve pays attention to it, too. It is a measure of behavior, whether all the buyers and sellers throughout the economy are really at it or if they're holding back. It is a measure of sentiment. Are the buyers comfortable or worried, or maybe about to panic? When they're worried the money flow slows, economic activity slows, and we all end up with a little less than we might otherwise have.

Buyers often aren't rational. They're more fickle than sellers. They calculate risk, and they get it wrong. Buyers and sellers miscalculate risk. Billionaires do that, too. But one thing that sets them apart is they aren't hungry, not driven to invest for another million or hundred million, and they know from experience that a miss on the risky side can be quite painful. So, they adjust, get more cautious and choose to not invest their hoard. The money doesn't get put to work the way it would in the hands of the eager, hungry, free-market entrepreneur envisioned by economist Adam Smith. The money is hoarded rather than invested. The economy underperforms, and we all lose a bit of what our little share could have otherwise returned. Some of that passive money should be pushed back to work. In the hoarded pile it is useless, but when extracted and set to work building infrastructure, both public and private, and human capital, it transforms into real wealth.

[1] https://www.archives.gov/milestone-documents/servicemens-readjustment-act

CHAPTER 11

BILLIONAIRES. WHY DO WE HAVE THEM?

Awe.

In 1759, University of Glasgow scholar Adam Smith published the first of his two famous works, The Theory of Moral Sentiments. Not nearly as often quoted as another work from a decade and a half later, The Wealth of Nations, it is still a useful reference for insights about human behavior. Smith tried to explain why humans do what they do. He offered his "impartial spectator" as a mentor, one to suggest what we ought to do.

In one discussion, "Of the origin of Ambition and the distinction of Ranks," he observes that people, even when their own station is low, turn out for the parade. They derive pleasure from just the sight of wealth and success on display. They seem to want to be awed by figures of authority in the parade, especially those wearing colorful and shiny symbols of status. People will worship their king when he's alive and mourn when he dies. Some will weep even if he ruled as a tyrant.

Today we don't have kings, at least in a traditional sense. Donald Trump's eagerness to decorate with gold, the genuine shiny metal of royalty, is an aberration. But Trump is an actor, a pretender. He's not the real thing. And he's not a "real" billionaire.

Today's kings are the real billionaires, or vice versa. They are extraordinary, and most folks know that, although probably not fully comprehending how extraordinary. We are awed by the extraordinary. Consistent with Smith's observations from 300 years ago we defer to these kings, even bow down to them. Could it be we seem to want them because of some inherent human attraction or curiosity about the unusual? Could it be the attraction isn't actually to the mortal standing beside the stack of money, but rather to the stack?

Maybe as humans we are just attracted to any shiny thing standing out against the dark gray of everyday life. That would make sense as an evolutionary survival strategy mechanism. Think of our fascination with beautiful sunsets and that we remember that ancient saying, "red sky at morning, sailor take warning." Or imagine a primitive forager seeing a small splash of color in the distance, standing out from the green. It could be a protein meal for the tribe back at camp, or a predator, or a patch of berries. We may have billionaires partly because the unusual catches our eye. We want them for the parade. There's a certain rush when we encounter exceptional beauty or exceptional anything else, including extreme piles of money.

Gravity.

Attributing a physical phenomenon like gravity to money is fanciful of course, except for money's observable tendency to clump, what real matter does. Bits of it are attracted to other bits, and bigger masses overwhelm the pull of the smaller. When a pile of money gets to a certain size, it seems like any strip of it floating by gets sucked right in. Economists identify it as a tendency toward monopoly. Gravity it seems, would ultimately collapse the whole thing into a black hole, unless there is some method for stirring the pot, or some kind of spinning motion to intervene and keep the clumps from getting too big. Carried to the extreme, with no one stirring, gravity could suck the money into one giant clump in the hands of a trillionaire with none in the hands of anybody else. Collapse. Doubtful that would be good for anybody, even the one monopolist, the one of the "greediest sons-a-bitches..." who "want it all," and who ended up with it all.

Drift.

Lazy rich people become more risk averse, so the money in the pile is more likely to stay there instead of being put to use by the hungry, energetic, entrepreneurial types farther down the chain. Caution and unwillingness to invest makes extraordinary loss for those lazy ones at the top less likely. Once they become exceedingly wealthy, they tend not to self-destruct. There's a low attrition rate. They drift but don't die off quickly.

It isn't just the billionaires who are lazy, however. It may be that the pot stirrers have fallen asleep. Stirring means actively directing some of the money flow, exerting force against the money gravity. It means taking a significant portion of that flow in taxes, particularly of the clumps accelerating quickly toward the already huge piles. In previous times more than 50% of the flow was redirected. Radical as that sounds, the radical pileup, one enormous stack with none for anyone else, that seems inevitable without intervention, would be quite unpleasant in comparison.

The pot stirring has to be mandated. It must be the law that taxes are collected. There must be a tax collector to carry out the mandate.

But laws are written by Congress, and it seems that body is unwilling to, or too lazy to do their pot stirring duty. Makes you wonder if there's a deal. Makes you wonder if there have been words like, "just leave the money stacks alone, and we'll leave you alone. Your office was hard to get. Pretty sure you'd like to keep it."

Courtiers

Louis XIV, the Sun King, was the grandest of them all. His Versailles Palace is now a World Heritage Site, visited by 15 million tourists each year. In its (his) time, a couple generations before the French Revolution [1] took away the crown and the head of his great-great-grandson, the then king Louis XVI, and shortly after, his wife, "let them eat cake" Marie Antoinette, Versailles was the place to be, maybe "the place" in all of Europe. Louis Quatorze, reared as a royal, apparently looked the part and embraced the role he played, on the throne for 72 years. He was powerful and glamorous, and he welcomed the "beautiful people" to keep him company. The courtiers, lesser-noble suck-ups of the time, crowded in to be close and put up with what historians report as not luxury living conditions.

Louis lived in luxury, his companions not so much. They pretended and performed in his spectacle, being there in fancy dress when needed, and always subservient. They came for favors. The king was the only one who could grant them.

The courtiers of Versailles were historically exceptional, certainly in part because the king was exceptional, and he had the money. For 72 years running, if you wanted a deal, this was the place to get it. It is likely that three generations of some families, the rich and powerful, or almost so, French aristocrats, went or sent their titled agents…with palm out. And they displayed reverence for, and loyalty to, the Sun King.

Spectacular as Versailles was, in one respect it really was not unusual. There have probably always been courtiers, the hangers on and thieves who know where to go, that know just like Willie Sutton, the most quoted bank robber in history, who answered so clearly and logically when asked why he robbed banks, "because that's where the money is." Guess where the money is now.

Even more than the Sun King.

If you answered in the stacks with the billionaires, good, you've followed this narrative so far. But you wouldn't be quite right. A much bigger stack is in Washington, D.C. It's the U.S. Government's take from taxes. And a fresh stack drops into town every year. If the richest ten in the US put all their money into one pile it would amount to perhaps two and a half trillion dollars. Every year the U.S. Treasury takes in double that, and Congress and the President argue and then agree to borrow and spend an additional two trillion. It's a $7 trillion pile that renews every year. That's 7,000 billion dollars.

Do you suppose there might be a few courtiers, and a couple Willie Sutton wannabes hanging out somewhere along or close to

Pennsylvania Avenue? Could you imagine two guys sitting at the bar at the Old Ebbitt Grill,[2] a block from the White House, joking about getting their hands on just one of those seven thousand? Can you imagine after a couple drinks the voices get a bit lower, and they keep talking.

Three blocks north is K Street. In the United States there are 13,000 lobbyists, and K Street is their hive. The street crosses Pennsylvania Avenue a few blocks west of the White House. The U.S. Capitol Building is in the opposite direction. K goes east, and Pennsylvania Avenue angles away. The street passes about nine blocks from the Capitol, a ten-minute walk for the K Street guys to the Senators and Representatives, and that $7 trillion pile of money.

Of course, not all who come to the Nation's Capital are working on behalf of a billionaire trying to protect his stash. People petition their government, they lobby for action on all kinds of issues, like clean drinking water and safe and fair working conditions, and a habitable environment for the earth's human residents six generations in the future. There are good works to be done and they usually need money. And there are competing interests. For example, addressing my concern for those kids in the future may hurt you if the rules get changed, and your job in an oilfield or coal mine gets eliminated.

It's not always a pretty process what happens in Washington. Some liken it to what goes on in a sausage factory. Fried up, the stuff comes out of the pan delicious, but not so savory is the trip from the hog pen to the pan. The sausage making of governing is sometimes smelly compromise, but it's how humans survive without killing each other.

The problem in Washington is that those with the most have so much more, much more power and influence. For a pittance they can guide, or maybe even do the writing for the tax law writers.

Larger lobbying firms report annual revenues of $50 million. Approximately 30 individuals in the United States each have $50 billion in their money pile. Any of them could spend just one billion, 2% of their hoard and pay the salaries of every employee and the partners in those K Street firms, twenty of the top ones with their hundreds of lawyers. There may well be more lobby lawyers than there are elected law writers, and if you're a billionaire their services are not that expensive.

That same 2% of the dollar pile could finance 100 congressional election campaigns. Have no doubt the election winning courtiers know who pays their rent. The billionaires will stay billionaires. We'll have them until voters throw out the puppet courtiers, along with the king. We may have to replace both with an entirely new crew more willing to stir the pot.

---

[1] French Revolution 1789 https://www.history.com/articles/french-revolution

[2] https://www.ebbitt.com

CHAPTER 12

PEACE AND PROSPERITY.

Mother Nature.

It is doubtful people ever lived expecting peace and prosperity uninterrupted in their lifetimes and extending a couple generations into the future. Calm may have always been the exceptional interlude between crises and threats, those being inevitable thanks to Mother Nature...and to other humans.

Our era is no different...except for two threats of our own making that are truly existential. We have the capability to wipe away all of humanity with nuclear weapons. Thanks to luck or Providential Mercy we've survived so far without accident or mass-scale malice that could have ended us, kind of an amazing 80 years since the destruction of Hiroshima. It's doubtful Mother Nature cares one whit if we keep going for another 80 years or 800.

The other existential threat is climate change. One can argue whether it is the most immediate danger; the climate fatal outcome is likely multiple generations in the future. Urgency is a harder sell when ultimate tragedy falls on ones we will never know, the grandchildren of the grandchildren of our grandchildren. It is a hard sell, too, because this crisis competes for our attention with other immediate ones. Also, the messengers who warn us of the coming disaster are discounted partly because some of them seem unwilling to acknowledge the possibility that we could innovate ourselves back away slightly from the worst possible outcomes.

We can't perceive the future. We only speculate, make our best guess. We must do that knowing full well that we don't have a perfect understanding of Mother Nature. She will continue to surprise us. But we do know her world, the one we live in, well enough to do some speculation with confidence. We know our educated-guess-future is closer to the real future than what we would predict based on a coin toss. We do way better than a 50% chance of getting it right.

Now the most highly regarded students of nature, particularly that aspect of it we call climate, are in almost universal agreement that our human activities are driving a rise in temperature that will cause abandonment of vast areas of the earth long populated by humans. They predict loss of life and mass migration by the end of this century. It will get worse in the next century and beyond unless we stop altering our protective blanket atmosphere.

Human Nature.

The other nature we have some understanding of is our own. We have written accounts from at least the last five or six thousand years. The record is replete with examples of human mistakes and folly. It is our nature to make mistakes. Wars with weapons, puny in comparison to today's nukes, killed millions in the two world wars in the first half of the twentieth century. Sobering to contemplate the odds of us never again making mistakes like the ones that led to those disasters. Frighteningly slim many believe, on our current path.

But what if we could change the odds to be more in our favor? Should we try? Of course we should. Pushing to change direction, to change the odds is every bit a normal human behavior just as imbedded in us as is showing kindness, or being cruel, sometimes being the fool, and sometimes following the fool. We should try to change the odds, and we have, or can have, agency to do so.

However, our species suffers from a fundamental evolutionary failure or incompleteness that complicates our present challenge. There are 8 billion of us and we all interpret threats and opportunities around us slightly differently. Some dismiss threats bearing down on them (or us) even when the calculation of a neutral observer, Adam Smith's "impartial spectator" for example, would predict a 90% chance of disaster. Others just don't have the mental capacity to make the calculation, and some make it but don't care. Some are the "greediest sons-a-bitches that want it all" who will take it all and will take agency from the other 7,999,999,999 of us. They want the money and do not consider anything else. They will not make decisions to improve the odds of our surviving the two existential challenges of our time. We have technology that can and will kill us unless we improve our odds, but we haven't evolved to the point that agency automatically falls into the hands of those most inclined to improve the odds. In our moment it seems agency just follows the money, sucked in by the gravity.

But we are not doomed. We fall victim to folly and greed and extreme malice, but not always. Surely, if history was a complete record, it would reveal many examples of when stupidity at the top could have resulted in disaster but didn't. We would read of the Trojan Horse not being rolled through the fortress gate. How might that different story have happened?

Collective insight.

It could be that another of our evolved human nature behaviors is the often-too-slow eventual development of collective insight, a realization that there is a lunatic in charge, the decision maker. The king is crazy, and he will lead the tribe off a cliff if not stopped.

An interesting thing about collective insight is that it is kind of like money in one way. It clumps. It might start with a couple guys on lunch break simultaneously smirking after seeing a glimpse of idiocy on a TV in the corner of the room. Or maybe it's a couple bored women at a company holiday party, a bit relaxed after two glasses of wine as they contemplate a third. Genuine human one to one contact can energize, and even after the dulling effects of the alcohol, or maybe because of the dulling effects, real connection starts to form. And the real stuff, including the ever-present annoyance of the phony stuff coming from the screen that causes a smile or grimace, starts to flow. The king is on that screen, and everybody knows the king is a dangerous clown, a brutal idiot some would say, and the world is an unpleasant mess that will only get worse until he's gone. But what to do?

The conspiracy starts jokingly at first. It could be a sci-fi scenario, like the villain accepting a phony call-back to his home galaxy and instantly being teleported away from earth, maybe in the opposite direction from the galaxy that called. Or maybe it would be something more mundane, like a bolder loosened by the spring thaw, falling perfectly timed to crash on top of his car as he motorcades to a campaign event in West Virginia. Better for a laugh would be his demise triggered by something to do with sex or vanity.

It would start with a good laugh, the humor partially tempering the stronger emotions underneath, disgust, and probably fear. The hilarity might fade a bit, and the conversation continue, a bit darker.

Some conversations don't start with the good laugh, instead a glance from one slave, or beggar, to another that says, "You knock him down. I'll grab the stuff." Another clump forms, of insight, the condensation nucleus of this one, near starvation.

When deprivation becomes visible on every street the clumps form by the thousands, and then maybe tens of thousands, and they gravitate. In the worst case it becomes a mob of hundreds of thousands, it turns toward the castle, and the tyrant refuses to acknowledge that it's the end. Some of the guards recognize it and run. They survive. Those who stay, and the courtiers, perish in the flames. It is a violent mutiny, and the king is deposed. Death and destruction very likely spreads way beyond the castle walls.

But could there be an alternative collective insight? Could one be forming now that could pull us back from that worst case, and the even "more-worst" case scenarios, the twin threats of nuclear annihilation and climate annihilation? What if some of the courtiers could be pulled into the survival camp? What if some of the billionaires aren't actually the greediest SOBs, and what if they already recognize their own survival depends on avoiding castle conflagration catastrophe?

If we don't pull back a pitchforks-in-the-streets, French Revolution style, anarchy-runaway is possible. That could be the ultimate endgame for the inequality that seems to be on an accelerating trajectory toward extreme.

A revolution might not significantly alter the climate path, but it certainly could heighten the risk of nuclear loss of control. If the anarchists who want to burn it all down succeed, also consumed in the fire might be any succeeding leader we would prefer for the finger on the nuclear trigger. In the aftermath, as the smoke clears, the one at the top may as likely as not be another lunatic, as bad or worse than the one violently removed at the start of the conflagration. The rampage will be awful, and after it the world will be even less safe than before.

The Worried Billionaires

JPMorgan Chase CEO Jamie Dimon, speaking at the World Economic Forum meeting in Davos, Switzerland in January 2026, suggested higher taxes for the rich as a way to reduce the federal government debt risk to the larger US economy.[1]

Mitt Romney, US Senator from Utah, Republican candidate for President in 2012, and before that, conservative Governor of the liberal state of Massachusetts, argued for the same in an editorial in the New York Times in December 2025.[2]

Romney became wealthy previously as a founder and manager of Bain Capital, a large global private investment firm. He is reportedly a bit short of the billionaire club, his net worth measured in just hundreds of millions, but he's certainly part of the who's who for any conversation about wealth.

Others, including Warren Buffett, Bill Gates, MacKenzie Scott, Mark Cuban, and George Soros have spoken, and acted, in recognition of the dangerous wealth gap between the ultra-rich and everybody else. They've all recognized that they have too much money.

In his classic work The Theory of Moral Sentiments, Adam Smith suggests that "the pleasures of vanity and superiority are seldom consistent with perfect tranquility, the principle and foundation of all real and satisfactory enjoyment." He recounts, "The inscription upon the tombstone of the man who had endeavored to mend a tolerable constitution by taking a physic; '*I was well, I wished to be better; here I am*' may generally be applied with great justness to the distress of disappointed avarice and ambition."

It could be some of the extraordinarily wealthy today are already in a search for tranquility.

The case against the extreme wealth concentration is strong. At the no-wealth end people suffer deprivation and continuous stress, even worrying about not having access to food, or a place of shelter from the elements. Up just a notch from the bottom, insecurity is the norm because employment is usually "at the will of the employer," and if a worker suffers illness, he or she will very likely suffer unemployment, and very soon after, poverty. Sick and no money. The reality is that for a very large part of America, including working America, there is minimal or no safety net. There is certainly a feeling of no safety net.

At the other extreme life may not be so great, either. A few, like MacKenzie Scott and George Soros stand out because of their very public efforts to use their wealth to find solutions to humanity's big problems, but they are the exception. Most seem uninterested in anything other than the money and perhaps keeping a low profile because they know, whether or not they are a thief themselves, there are thieves, and the thieves carry knives. Strolling the neighborhood with a bag of gold is dangerous.

So, folks at the lower end, the lower half, and those at the very top aren't enjoying the full benefits of our modern economy. Half fear an early demise from starvation, and the very few at the top fear a knife in the back. What about the rest in the top half?

Some are doing well. Happiest are probably the ones who realized at a fairly young age that chasing wealth for its own sake just wasn't as interesting as pursuing some other curiosity of nature, or developing a skill closer to an art, or simply collaborating with others to just get the community's everyday housekeeping chores done. Some who take one of these paths also become wealthy. They do well while doing good. Living with, and recognizing that they have plenty, while continuing to be a productive member of the tribe, would be admirable in the eyes of philosopher Adam Smith's "impartial spectator."

But even those in this most enviable position must sometimes feel discomfort. They may be comfortable now but likely wonder what the future holds for their children or grandchildren. Quite likely they understand their own success followed a long period of investment in education and specialized training. It is also quite likely they grasp the reality that the United States is sliding behind China and losing ground relative to economies in other parts of the world. They may worry that their progeny aren't being prepared for their future. This cohort, much of that top half, as well as many farther below on the wealth distribution are uncomfortable knowing that investments directed now at a better world for their children, and the children to come, are inadequate.

---

[1] https://fortune.com/2026/01/21/jamie-dimon-davos-making-world-better-place/

[2] https://www.nytimes.com/2025/12/19/opinion/romney-tax-the-rich.html

CHAPTER 13

AI, MOTHER NATURE, AND MONEY.

Winter

The January snowstorm was a mess for half the country. On the southern side of its track, it was ice on everything, beautiful to look at but destructive. Some people died from accidents and a few from hypothermia. Ice storms take out electric service. No electric? No heat. The heat pump won't run without electricity, and neither will the oil burner or gas furnace.

Farther to the northeast it was snow. First person account, two feet of the beautiful stuff to shovel...just to get out of the house. Fortunately, it was the light and fluffy kind so no trees crashing and taking down power lines. Mostly just inconvenience here, where it's normal in winter for every third truck to have a plow attached. We can still go when we want to, but it's slow, and lots of places like schools are closed.

But this weather system was a bit more of an attention getter because quite low temperatures came with it. Minnesota reported a wind chill temperature of -40F, and that bitter cold spread eastward with the airmass. It froze pipes, including ones that carry natural gas to power generating plants. Ironically, it wasn't snow on solar panels but rather ice in gas lines that put hundreds of thousands of utility customers in the dark. There wasn't enough power to keep folks in the light and warm. A million homes and other electricity users suffered a blackout as the storm rolled through the southeast and Mid-Atlantic states.

Ironic, too, problems like this have been predicted because of the huge new demands of AI data centers...to keep them cool. A contrarian thinker might wonder why if it's so cold outside, cooling a computer is such a big deal, and if AI is so smart, and it's now helping us with everything, why didn't it help keep the lights on? If you're one of the AI worriers or tech Luddites, or a bit grumpy about the whole thing for your own reasons, you might ask why "it" didn't keep the lights on. And that brings us back to the core of this essay, the money chase and where that money goes or doesn't go, into piles that are already too big or alternatively, into needed genuine investment, like grid upgrades.

Double trouble.

We have two major transformations going on simultaneously, the one mandated by Mother Nature, her chemistry and physics telling us we are toast if we don't stop pumping CO_2 into our protective blanket, and the other a near quantum leap in what is possible and what we expect from our computers. Both require significant investment.

We have a viable path for the climate-CO_2 challenge. The technology part of this path is ready now, and investment to install it becomes cashflow positive almost immediately. However...

Complicating our path for survival against climate doom is the fact that the monster computer requires a monster jump in the energy used to compute and to keep it cool. It runs on electricity as does a major tech piece for the transition away from carbon combustion transportation, the electric motor. Both transformations are competing for electrical energy. Both are competing for investment capital. As always, there isn't an infinite supply of money to invest. Do you suppose there's potential for mistake or mischief in this not-so-little competition, or maybe more accurately, money-scramble of the decade?

There are hints of mistake. To some eyes the AI ruckus looks like a classic gold rush or tulip-bulb mania. The top ten companies most engaged in artificial intelligence have a market capitalization of about $20 trillion. Nvidia is the top dog, and the stock market thinks it is worth over $4 trillion. That's 4,000 billion dollars. The price suggests some think the company will generate net income of $1,000,000,000 every year for the next 4,000 years, or $40,000,000,000 every year for the next 100 years, or $400,000,000,000 every year for the next ten years. That last number is about what the top three companies, Alphabet (Google), Apple, and Microsoft combined, earned in 2025. There definitely is optimism and enthusiasm. The thing is, artificial intelligence is real. It delivers real value. But…"artificial" is real? Hmm...that market value, real value? Might there also be some FOMO?[1]

Investors and speculators are in love with AI, and Nvidia *is* making money selling its products and services, but not *that much* money. If you buy the stock at its current price your share of reported earnings works out to about a one and a half percent annual return, about a third what you'd get from an old fashioned, much safer, certificate of deposit from your bank.

Yes, to our wiser angels.

We are making progress aligning with the climate mandate in some of our activities. And most of the newer gadgets we use are more efficient. Electricity produced with solar panels in many places where people live results in about one tenth as much carbon being put up. It's usually cheaper, too, so there's reason for optimism. The possibility of a nice return on investment suggests a very timely Mother Nature and money synergy.

There's good news on transportation, as well. Electric vehicles, even if half their energy comes from fossil fuel power plants, are responsible for far less greenhouse gas pollution, probably a fifth as much or less than what their internal combustion counterparts put out. Even air transportation is cleaner. The latest generation airliners like the Boeing 787, deliver about 90 seat-miles per gallon of fuel.[2] It's predecessor from fifty years ago, the Boeing 727 used about triple that per seat. It got about 30 seat-miles per gallon. This writer spent a lot of hours as a pilot in the cockpit of that plane and can attest there were many flights with many empty seats. Breakeven load factor, the percentage of seats filled, for an airline then, was typically in the range of 50-60%, so there were empty seats, in marked contrast with air travel today when they're mostly full. Someone traveling by air in 1976 was doing it at something close to 15 or 20 miles per gallon. In 2026 it is closer to 60 or 80 miles per gallon.

The carbon footprint isn't as good as walking or a bicycle or doing it in an EV. The electric would get you the equivalent of 125 or 150, or double that if there were two of you in the car. But it would take you three days instead of three hours. You could do it in your trusty old gas(oline) burner at 25 mpg and three days, too. No over-water, of course.

Some of our other gadgets are significantly improved, as well. Heat pumps work, and their efficiencies are much better than they used to be. And how about those lights? LEDs are amazingly good compared to their predecessors. Use your LED lamp for four hours a day and it should last ten years, and it uses way less electricity than Edison's miracle bulb. His gadget from almost 150 years ago was amazing. It was much less likely to set the house on fire than the gas lamp or kerosene lamp that it replaced, and you could bring light to the whole room by simply pushing the switch button on the wall. But the bulb was awful in terms of efficiency. Folks, including Thomas Edison, thought he had invented a light, but the reality is he had invented a heater that happens to give off a little light. 95% of the energy it uses comes out of the bulb as waste heat, a meager 5% illuminates.

AI fork in the road.

AI energy needs do handicap our effort to slow the excess carbon dioxide buildup. The most troubling future scenario would be for all the clean energy coming available, thanks to solar panels and windmills, gobbled by *exascale* computers as they displace every working human. Or it could be even more of a setback if the machines cause fossil fuel consumption rates to resume their climb. What a dystopian future it could be, all the information and knowledge workers excessed and sent back to the oil fields and mines to physically labor extracting ancient fossil remains to feed their AI masters.

Another possible reality is not so grim. It could be that imbedded in the AI hype are grossly overstated future energy needs. Evidence of the uncertainty in this early part of the story was the impact of news of efficiency gains reported by a Chinese relative newcomer in early 2025. That company, DeepSeek, was thought to be producing useful artificial-intelligence-generated information using about half as much energy as other models, many of those using chips manufactured by companies like Nvidia. Panic resulted and the Nvidia stock price cratered.[3] The one-day loss of market value was a record $590 billion. You might surmise that multi-trillion-dollar stack of money representing the perceived value of Nvidia had grown a bit tippy. The pile wobbled and some chunks of it fell off the top.

The panic didn't last, though. A year later that reality check seems way distant in the mirror. Market confidence has returned. Company president, Jensen Huang, and President Trump made nice with each other, the Nvidia chips that were subject to some US-China angst were given a green light, and the market fell in love again, apparently deciding there could be some deep fake in that DeepSeek story. Optimists outnumber the pessimists, and the price per share is back near its all-time high.

Crypto.

There's another part to this story of push and shove with Mother Nature. She warns that unless we change our ways her place will again be populated by reptiles comfortable in way warmer temperatures and maybe plants gone wild loving the air with way more CO_2. Humans won't inhabit Earth. She's warning we have to stop burning fossil fuel and putting its residue into the air. This chapter, or maybe it's just a page, is a about the fact that a lot of energy is used to create digital currency, at least some types, like Bitcoin. Exactly how much isn't a simple calculation, and it is likely that some who have done the best at that number crunching aren't eager to share their findings. What we know is that a coin becomes one after a huge number of computer calculations, random number checks that make the discovery. Estimates for the amount of electricity consumed to make a coin vary from a half million kilowatt-hours to a million and a half, enough to power a hundred homes for a year. How much consumed is variable by location, too, and environmental impact is significantly lower if the electricity comes from renewable sources.[4]

Digital currencies have negative environmental impact. Exactly how serious an impact is perhaps harder to quantify because the technology offers its secrecy as a core selling point. Illicit trade and traders, engaged in activities prohibited in most societies, embraced the technology early on because no transaction records were created. Big drug deals, for example, could go down successfully, and the cops would have no money trail to follow. Utility was and is a real-value feature for some commercial activity, both good and bad. Environmental impact is hard to quantify partly because it is hard to quantify how big the whole phenomenon is. Precision isn't essential, however, to recognize there is serious impact. Another number that won't get you laughed out of the room, three or four trillion dollars worldwide is tied up in this trade.

The bigger problem is Mother Nature is competing against money for our attention and love. There's almost $10 Trillion pulled into the total fossil fuel enterprise every year. Worldwide it's surely millions of people engaged in it and dependent on that money flow to keep a roof over their heads and food on the table. Ten percent as your estimate of the total world economy devoted to satisfying our need for energy would probably sound reasonable to others who have made the calculation. If a fourth of the world's population is employed, i.e., the total worker-bee force, that means 2 billion people. Ten percent of that workforce is 200,000,000. If half of those are already on the clean energy side, a very generous assumption, you still have a hundred million humans working in conflict with Mother Nature's mandate. The other thing is some of those dragging their feet to slow the move to the clean side have really big piles of money. Just a small scoop from one of those piles can buy a legislator, or a whole bunch of them.

Mother Nature against money: Are we witness to, or in, a fight to the death? Is it money trying to kill us? And what exactly is it, money? The answer to that question is hiding in a puzzle almost as challenging as "artificial intelligence."

Money.

The phenomenon has been around for at least as long as humans have kept written records. Exactly what medium, beads, salt, pelts or gold coins, or a piece of paper with a picture of some famous good or evil person on it, called a pound, lira, euro, renminbi, or dollar, isn't that important. What matters is that money is very useful and very dangerous. No human is self-sufficient, and there may have never been one who survived for long without trading. "You got stuff I need, and I got stuff you need. Let's swap." It was simple barter at first, "Give me some of those berries, and I'll give you one of these fish. Better dinner for both of us."

Barter works okay for some things. Kids learn to do it pretty early on, like maybe at about age two. They get very good at negotiating with mom or dad. For bigger trades, the method just isn't adequate. Enter money—and very soon after that, banks and bank robbers. And then wannabe robbers who find clever ways to get the money without a gun and the likelihood of going to jail. Some end up billionaires.

Back to the question, what is money? In Econ 101 we were told it is a medium of exchange, a store of value, and a measure of account. And it's not just the paper stuff and metal coins. In fact, the bills and coins in the pocket are fairly trivial for most of us. The much bigger part we never touch or see, what we can tap into and send to almost any place in the world with a couple keystrokes or taps on the smartphone. Bank regulators try to keep track of the whole thing, and they can create more money or take it back, also with just a couple keystrokes.

Measure of account is interesting. We use money as a way to describe the size or value of something else, $4.99 equals a pound of grapes, for example. Or tell a friend that dinner for two is about a hundred bucks, and they will have a pretty good idea what to expect should they give your restaurant recommendation a try. The communication shortcut works well if the money, the currency, is a relatively stable one, like the official US dollar, the one guarded by the Federal Reserve. Of course, there is a shelf life for the number you give your friend. If they wait five years to try your dining spot, best plan $120.

The Fed regulates the supply of money, which has a direct impact on what we experience as inflation. It generally has mission success, gets close to its 2% target, but the actual number is usually a bit higher. Maybe best figure $5.15 for the grapes next year and $5.99 a couple years after that.

But how about those other forms of money, you know, doubloons and pieces of eight, or Bitcoin. The first two went the way of the Spanish Armada and sailing ship pirates centuries ago, so not of particular interest here. But what about Bitcoin and Ethereum, and all those other digital currencies, thousands of them, and lately quite a few with the Trump brand somehow attached? How do they compare to a good old hundred-dollar bill with Ben Franklin's image on the front? And how about gold?

Well, it turns out you could have done very well if you'd exchanged 15 of your Benjamins for an Ethereum coin in early April 2025, especially if you switched back in August. Triple your money!

It wasn't so good if you were the buyer in the middle of summer. Imagine having to explain to your spouse and kids that the almost $5,000 for the sunny-south beach trip at Christmastime and some shopping money that you "invested" was now worth half as much. It wouldn't have been too pleasant, either, if your mistake was with the set aside grocery money needed until the tax refund check shows up in April. Ethereum on August 23rd was $4,830. It was $2,764 on November 22nd.

Bitcoin fans have had quite a ride too. The cheerleaders predict the sky, $200,000, $1,000,000. There are believers. Some paid $124,310 on October 7th, 2025. They watched their coins crash to $84,209 on November 22nd. By early February it was below $70,000. Ouch!

Precious metal.

And how about the "gold standard," gold? Pretty wild here, too. The precious metal was actually quite stable through most of the Biden Presidency, hovering below $2,000 per ounce. There was no gold rush during the pandemic or when the Fed opened the faucets wide to bump up the money supply, and there were huge infrastructure-building initiatives, investments and Federal spending for economic stimulus. Through it all, gold was boring. It was...at least until the approaching election in 2024. If you held some gold then, as it looked more and more likely voters would choose a bit more excitement over tranquility for the next four years, you were happy to watch your bullion go pretty quickly from $2,000 right up to $2,500, a nice 25% gain in just a couple months. If you maintained your own tranquility and kept the gold in your vault through the first year of the new regime's excitement, or maybe you were just a bit sleepy...and then very lucky with your timing when you exchanged your gold back into official US currency, you did very, very well. If by dumb luck or extreme brilliance you bought your precious metal on February 16th, 2024, at $2,024 (not a misprint) and sold on January 29th, 2026 for $5,615, you hit a home run, a $3,591 gain, 177%.

There is the other side, though, the other side of luck. The odds in this casino are much better than Las Vegas or Atlantic City, partly because the cut for the house is way smaller, but it is essentially a zero-sum game. There are always losers. Imagine you bought at the peak on that wild January day and paid $5,615 for your ounce of gold. Next day was panic and the price plunged to $4,767. What a punch in the gut! That day was definitely painful for some, but in the bigger picture it was likely quite visible evidence of a massive sigh of relief. President Trump's announced choice to be the next Chairman of the Federal Reserve Board was perceived to be less a yes-man or crazy man than some of the other names floating around as the likely nominee. The markets sensed the possibility of some relative tranquility and a bit less chaos coming from Washington. It could be the scared money trying to shelter in gold felt a little safer coming out of its cave.

Econ 101.

Medium of exchange, a store of value, and a measure of account, says Econ 101. Money works for us all the time. How many times a day do you complete a transaction that involves money? If you're a typical American it might be two or three or a half dozen, and you and the other party rarely if ever give any thought to doing the exchange any other way. Most of us use official money and we use it as a proxy for measure. We equate $4.99 with a pound of grapes or a Starbucks Latte with a sprinkle of fancy stuff added. If you say a hundred bucks worth of groceries, I have a pretty good idea of what you're describing. Again, official currency works well for communicating.

How does the dollar do with that other function, store of value? This is where it gets interesting and sometimes contentious. Inflation nibbles away at the value of the dollar bill. The nibble is usually barely noticeable because the money we get from other people generally increases at about the same pace as the money we have to pay other people. Of course there are exceptions to the general rule, like when bird flu kills whole flocks of chickens and the price of eggs then jumps from $4 to $8. That's a hit to the grocery budget, and it's a wonderful opportunity for some politicians. They can shout about the cost of groceries doubling and blame it on the other side's stupidity. As we all know, neither side of the aisle has a monopoly on stupid. 100% tariffs, anyone?

Inflation does nibble, but the Federal Reserve has done okay at keeping the nibble at a tolerable rate. In fact, it says officially it wants the rate to be 2%, and that's close to what we get most of the time. If you found a small box of twenties in the basement of grandma's house when cleaning out after she passed, it would still have purchasing power even if she'd stashed it there fifteen years ago when she first realized grandpa was acting weird and maybe getting a little dangerous with money. As a store of value, official money, the US dollar works just fine.

But how about those other monies, gold, Bitcoin, Ethereum? Saving for a downpayment on a house or your retirement, would you put that extra from your paycheck into an Ethereum account? Probably not. These alternative forms of "money" flunk at the store of value function. They're too volatile.

Are they convenient for transactions? No. I bet your supermarket doesn't take Bitcoin or any other digital "currencies." Bet it wouldn't go to well either, if you presented a slice of a gold coin that you calculated to be worth $1,000 and demanded $900 in change back for your $100 grocery buy.

And as a measure of account, that coin, the whole coin, is it equal to the whole produce section, perhaps? Who knows? Even gold, probably the best of the bunch long term, is a lousy alternative. None of the alternatives are very good, so why do we have them? Isn't it funny how that why question keeps coming back?

Maybe gold should be considered a little differently. It is physically real but scarce. Its scarcity has been known for centuries if not millennia. Its inertness is unusual. That means no oxidation on its surface. It stays shiny, and it is really good at conducting electricity. Shiny clean and a good conductor makes it functionally high value in electronics that demand high reliability. There is real value not dependent purely on a perception of value. The other thing that makes it different is that no electronic alchemy is going to suddenly undermine it. Gold mining means picks and shovels and bulldozers and bulldozer drivers, with quantifiable costs that put a floor under the price of gold. If your time horizon is fifty years, not five years or five months maybe it is okay as a store of value.

So back to the slightly abbreviated question, why crypto? Sort of like why billionaires? The other one, the next one, as it always does, lurks close in the shadows. So what?

---

[1] Fear Of Missing Out

[2] A plane with 270 seats burns about three gallons of fuel for each mile it travels

[3] https://www.digidop.com/blog/deepseek-vs-chatgpt

[4] https://solartechonline.com/blog/bitcoin-electricity-consumption-mining-2025/

CHAPTER 14

DIAGNOSIS AND PROGNOSIS.

Not looking good.

Any observer halfway skilled at making comparisons would see us not thriving. Economic performance measured against earlier periods of the country's own history, and against other countries now, is trending down. General well-being, or the term used by Adam Smith, tranquility, is not what Americans feel. There is angst and discontent. The bitterness of the MAGA movement, the crudeness common in public discourse, immigration enforcement campaigns with uncomfortably close to police-state methods and the energetic pushback against those, are all markers of a nation that is not in a happy, healthy, place. Some see it at war with itself.

By many objective measures we live well. Few suffer genuine hunger. Most have access to adequate nutrition delivered in a palatable form and with variety never enjoyed by humans in earlier times. The size of the homeless population is an embarrassment, but even those individuals who are essentially helpless and penniless can usually find shelter if they want it. We don't have workers assigned the task of gathering the corpses of people who died alone on the streets in the middle of the night. The vast majority of us live in permanently constructed housing that is well lit, kept comfortably warm in winter and cooled with conditioned air during the heat of summer. Virtually all have access to mobility that would have been unimaginable to predecessors of just a few generations ago. Killer communicable diseases are rare, COVID-19 a reminder that they are not completely a thing of the past, but even it, the pandemic, as disruptive as it was and disastrous for a few, ranks as very minor compared to those endured by slightly earlier modern humans.

But objective measures are not always the most important, and data gathered, collated for display and then distributed, always arrives with a lag. The numbers don't lie but often are delivered late, and perhaps partly for that reason are somewhat discounted. People's perception of reality is what motivates them. Their tranquility or angst is fueled by their senses, what they feel about the larger world around them, not the pixel level detail and false precision of datapoints.

Very importantly, there is more money to be made stoking angst, and we allow it. Tranquility isn't as profitable. Rupert Murdoch's media empire, with Fox News as its superstar, is exhibit number one for that reality.

Murdoch may be a villain or just an opportunist, a most successful one. He has many younger imitators whose gig, and for some, goal in life, is to stir the pot. Some are genuine anarchists. They make money and make life less comfortable for the rest of us.

But a bit of discomfort is not always a bad thing. If the campfire starts to feel too hot, we move back. If the fertile valley turns to desert, the discomfort of hunger forces the tribe to move. The survivor tribes move before the food runs out completely. When there is danger, we move away. When there is a problem, we move to remedy it.

The scolds serve us when they point to problems that we may be slow to recognize. Importantly, not all of the scolds and sentinels warning us now are in it just for the money. Some are genuinely alarmed by the data and feel they have no moral choice except to try to stir us to act. They agitate us to make us move. As destructive as the money-making opportunists are much of the time, they are not always wrong about dangers they point out.

The kids ain't right.

There is agreement about some of the real problems we face. Academic achievement of our children has declined relative to their peers in other countries and against their predecessors in our own country. Our kids just aren't joining adult world as well equipped as those growing up in other parts of the world. There's evidence they aren't as well prepared for evolving technology, and they aren't as well prepared either with essential skills for self-governance.

Borrow too much.

Our government has taken on financial obligations on a scale without peacetime precedent. National debt has reached more than 120% of gross domestic product.[1] The worriers warn that we burden future American taxpayers, our children and grandchildren, with an obligation to pay interest that will unfairly lessen their quality of life. They say it is unfair, and they also warn that current deficit spending trends portend potential economic catastrophe, a collapse of the whole financial system that could spread suffering more widely than anything experienced since the global collapse of the 1930s and its aftermath.

We're making it too warm.

Almost all who use science as their primary tool for understanding our natural world, the physical world that feeds us, provides us with the oxygen we need continuously, and the atmosphere blanket that protects us from the too intense energy emitted by the nuclear fusion ball around which we rotate, agree that we are approaching self-destruction with our continued use of fossil fuel. Climate change, global warming, is real, and we are causing it. We could slow the warming and eventually eliminate it as a threat to wellbeing, but we choose instead to deny the awful, possible future reality. We delay aggressive action to reduce emissions, steps that would improve chances for a more tranquil life for those coming in the generations after us. We are not making the investments that are urged now by the "impartial spectator."

We pay but stay sick.

We compete with the world with a cost of operation handicap. Healthcare costs in the US are nearly double those of other modern economies. By some estimates the incremental burden, how much more we pay, is about 8% of our gross domestic product compared with the competition. Even as we pay way more, health outcomes are worse than those in most other advanced societies. We pay

18% of GDP, while in the UK it's about 11%, France, Germany, Japan 12%, China 7%, Korea 10%, Brazil 9%.[2] We outspend by a wide margin, yet we rank poorly on measures of outcome, at about number 35 for infant mortality[3] and 61 for life expectancy.[4] For a country that pioneered much of modern medicine, our performance today is mediocre or worse. We have a failing health care system.

We don't make it here.

We no longer manufacture the physical things we use in everyday life. The one-trillion-dollar trade deficit has meaning for economists and politicians, but it is a pixel size datapoint for most consumers and voters. But consumers do know where a lot of their stuff comes from. Buy it on Amazon or at Walmart and quite likely its place of origin is on the other side of the Pacific. If it has wheels, it's a good bet at least some of its parts came from Mexico. It may have been assembled in Mexico. You and your neighbors aren't manufacturing, employed at the plant that used to provide work and a paycheck based on union negotiated rates that you would spend mostly in your own neighborhood. The plant is shuttered and rusting. On the other side of this lopsided picture, China reported a trade <u>surplus</u> in 2025 of $1.2 trillion dollars.

Precise quantification, and qualification, of the problem is a challenge. The feeling of vulnerability doesn't depend on precision, however. We are anxious because in our gut we know it is an unsustainable situation. If we keep sending away money, at some point the money will be gone. Then what?

Expensive energy is a handicap.

Or will the money be gone? One group says no. The fossil fuel advocates say not to worry; we can just dig more money out of the ground and exchange it for all the other things we need but no longer make for ourselves. They say the climate thing is a non-issue, mostly a hoax or a plot to stifle freedom, so it should be completely ignored. They also pretend to ignore the fact that what they offer as our source of money, carbon fuel, is becoming obsolete. It is pricy compared to its renewable energy successors. The world is telling the producers that $60/barrel is too much. The producers, at least in the US, know they can't produce for less than that.

The market will reveal the real hoax, and it will reveal the futility of the current US government's efforts to prop up an end-stage industry. The effort does slow the inevitable transition, and as the government supports the drillers it imposes avoidable costs on the American economy. Delayed adoption of lower cost renewable energy and more efficient use of energy manifests as a self-imposed handicap. Our leadership is stepping on the brake pedal as the competition races farther ahead

Danger in the disparity.

The most glaring symptom of decline, even if it is not terminal decline...maybe more accurately described as a symptom of serious illness, is the disparity in the distribution of the benefits, what is produced by the workings of this huge, complex economy. Even as there is slow growth, those at the very top of the distribution continue to do extremely well. They accumulate huge piles of money. At the other end, economic sluggishness or falling behind compared to our competitors is perceptible to students of economics but felt acutely by just a few in any given, relatively short time frame. The effects are cumulative, though. The number of those impacted grows, and the number who by mid-career have not been impacted by, or heard stories of, corporate downsizing, bankruptcies, and unfriendly takeovers, shrinks. More and more know of promised retirement benefits that disappeared into the ether, and more make the firsthand discovery that once surplused from the workforce, re-entry is very often at a much lower compensation rate.

The ranks of the disgruntled grow as the billionaires grow richer. Some of the disgruntled are desperate. Desperate people can be dangerous.

Not smooth ahead.

Unless there are course corrections, the decline will continue. If one is very generous and estimates our handicap at 10%, others will have a doubling of economic output compared to us in not much more than seven years. But ten percent may be too low a number. Health care 8%? Energy 5%? Lack of manufacturing efficiency 4%? And there is one more missing from the list above, excessive defense spending. We spend a percent or two of gross domestic product more than almost everybody else. Maybe when it's all added up, we're hobbled to the tune of 20%. If we managed to just hold on, not grow and not shrink, we'd watch our competitors race past us with a double in three years.

The prognosis is not good. America will fall farther behind. Discontent will grow because what is now perceptible to students of economics will become obvious to everyone. The fact that people in Europe and China, probably Brazil, maybe India, and other places are then living better than us, will sink in. More obvious to everyone, too, will be the wealth discrepancy. The scolds and rabble rousers will grow bolder at drawing attention to it. There will be names and faces more visibly attached to the biggest piles of money, and there will be the usual clamor for scapegoats. The current course could end with a violent shove on the rudder. Call it a revolution or class war, or just a very shocking leveling with plenty of destruction. The ship will roll, maybe not enough to completely capsize but surely enough to terrorize everybody on board. Don't forget that also in the mix is artificial intelligence, nuclear weapons, and the reality that there always are individuals hiding among us who are genuine psychopaths who would kill us all if given the chance. How can you not be worried about what could happen next? Another inconvenient but imaginable, less disastrous, scenario might be the captain with his wobbly compass runs this ship of state at flank speed onto the mudflats at high tide, and there it will stick, and we'll sit stuck, until rescued by Canada or Mexico or China, or somebody. Surely, getting steadier hands on the wheel now and making a gentler steering adjustment is preferable.

---

[1] https://fred.stlouisfed.org/series/GFDEGDQ188S

[2] https://data.worldbank.org/indicator/SH.XPD.CHEX.GD.ZS

[3] https://www.americashealthrankings.org/publications/reports/2023-annual-report/international-comparison

[4] https://www.worldometers.info/demographics/life-expectancy/

CHAPTER 15

HEADING CHANGE.

Stormy weather.

Our ship is in troubled waters with a dark sky ahead. There is light, but we're not pointed toward it. We need a change of direction, or the ride will get even rougher. Social unrest escalating to disaster seems a more real possibility today than at any time in the country's history. Unimaginable since the end of the Civil War, dissolution of the Union seems more plausible with each passing day of chaos in Washington. Some, maybe including the impartial spectator, see an even grimmer reality already, destruction by design, not pure chaos.

There could be a breakup. We have large population and economic centers where people who live there would look favorably to connecting with Canada and severing ties with parts of what is now the United States. Imagine how it would go if those folks were given that option or the alternative, sending their elected Representatives and Senators to meet in the new government offices when construction is complete, in the new United States Capital, in Texarkana, or Tulsa, or Houston.

And imagine the possibilities after a popular multi-lingual governor of California really connects with a popular multi-lingual President of Mexico as they celebrate synergies revealed following the recent removal of border bottlenecks at Tijuana and the old barrier there is replaced by a simple historical marker. Imagine an open trade highway running the entire west coast from the Oregon border all the way to Mexico City. Imagine the next logical step as benefits from the natural resources of that vast geography and the brainpower and muscle power of that large population collaborating, become obvious. Calmexico, Mexcalico, or Estados Unidos del Pacifico? Maybe Oregon would join, too, and Arizona. Farther to the east, Texas could still have its wall.

None of this is inevitable, unrest that escalates to mass destruction and loss of life, or complete failure and breakup of the Unites States. Our place as a nation is certainly significant in the long human story. It has been a contributor to what all but the most fringe of hermits consider progress, and even with our current embarrassments most would choose to preserve it. With a not uncomfortable turn to a new heading, not a rudder hardover, we can be on a new course, and we will track clear of disaster. We can avoid a conflagration, and we don't have to end this experiment in democracy that we call The United States of America.

The change we need is quite simple in concept. We need to move idle wealth, an idle accumulated surplus, and convert it into active and productive invested capital. Productive capital includes physical infrastructure, a shared knowledge base, and the knowledge base held in the head of each individual participant in the economy and in each participant in our governance process. We need to build the stuff we need…to build stuff, and we need to train every person to be a productive participant in our shared endeavor. We would be fools to not also direct some of that idle money to change our system for access to two of the most important and expensive items in our budget, energy and health. The opportunity, the potential payback from these two investments, is extraordinary, a higher quality life experience for all of us at significantly lower cost.

Invest in infrastructure, educate the workforce, reduce the cost of energy and health care. It's quite easy to say what we need to do to pull ourselves out of the slide and avoid what looks like an increasingly bleak future. Now to the hard part, putting it down on a doable list, a to-do list.

1. Pull some money out of the idle pot.

Too much money sits idle. One reason it sits is that when idle it isn't as visible to the tax collector, and especially for many of those most strongly motivated by money, avoiding paying any more than the absolute minimum to the government, is an almost religious understanding of prudence. Whether genuine prudence or simple greed is the real driver, over the last half century, tax law has been "adjusted" to accommodate the wishes of the wealthiest. Tax rates are radically lower. And accounting definitions changes allow a great deal of wealth accumulation to never be reported as income. The result is lower tax revenues and the tax burden being shifted to those who are already receiving a smaller share of the economy's output. People receiving lesser benefit are being required to pay a higher share of the expenses of the commonwealth, including for keeping up the infrastructure on which everyday life and all commerce depend. The wealthiest don't pay in proportion to the benefit they receive.

Heading change.

Evidence of too much money idling and not wisely invested includes current stock market valuations. By almost all measures, there is a high level of speculation. The flood of dollars exchanged for alternatives as vaporous as cryptocurrency is an indicator that too many people don't know what else to do with their money. They don't see or recognize other investment opportunities. The market is not revealing a channel for that excess money to flow to real investments that are needed. The Nvidia valuation that projects this artificial intelligence play to generate $40 billion of income each year for the next 100 years should be the blindingly bright flashing LED warning that the AI fervor or fever is now the tail wagging the dog. Markets are not doing well at allocating funds in the best long-term interest of the American people.

Pulling money back is not a task without risk, however. Smash and grab is rarely a tactic or strategy with good outcomes. Anarchists and thieves, maybe even greedier than the current holders of the gold, don't care about the rest of us and will swoop down on any opportunity. They will be happy to use us as participants in it, if they can get the riot started. Pulling money back is a crowd task. We must be careful to keep the crowd focused on the mission and not let it be taken over by rowdies.

Just yanking the money away from the billionaires would not be consistent either with our long-accepted standards of right and wrong, of fairness. We accept everyone's right to their life, liberty, and the pursuit of happiness, and we also honor their right to claim property. Just taking someone's property is not acceptable. Taxes must be collected but done with care. Making them proportional to benefit received, fairness, should be the goal. Reference to earlier versions of the tax code can help guide a rewrite. Meeting the nation's real investment needs is the mission.

2. Build roads, bridges, and factories.

Roads with a smooth surface and bridges where needed to make the through speed and travel time feel efficient are an easy sell. And only a few who worry the most about cars going too fast say no to fixing potholes in the street.

Almost everybody would say yes to manufacturing in the hometown. Siting the production line to build kitchen appliances on an unused lot in a commercial-industrial park at home rather than making that site a distribution center for appliances manufactured in Asia or South America or Africa would be cheered. Making it a place for the kid next door, or your nephew who is bored and now spends too much time watching influencers on YouTube or watching in awe and wishing he could be in the game with ether coins, to instead be at the controls running the robots on that manufacturing line, and be well paid for being there doing it, would be way preferable. Knowing that factory will pay taxes here to support the services that "our town" provides its citizens, instead of paying some other place, is much preferred by almost everybody, too.

Few would complain if investment in clean energy distribution infrastructure results in less money spent every month on the electric bill. Almost everybody would choose clean, too.

3. Keep the kids in school.

At the turn (the beginning) of the last century a lot of kids didn't get a full twelve years of schooling. A farm boy who finished eighth grade could be just as useful walking behind a plow pulled by a couple mules as one who made it through twelfth. The one who joined work world sooner, full time, likely had odds for success nearly as good as the one who graduated from high school. Twelve years was enough, or maybe more than enough.

Now it's not enough. There's just so much more to learn. The mule has been replaced by a machine that can do a hundred times as much work, but it can be just as cantankerous, and its complexity can render it useless quickly unless managed by someone with reading skills, maybe math skills, and for sure, an understanding of how to communicate with and use computers. And physical strength, so useful when work is about moving things with human muscle, is now not nearly as valuable as brain strength and skill, in almost all enterprises. There are few places on earth where a kid behind a draft animal is a very important contributor to the economy. For sure, America's competitors are preparing their next generations with science skills, math skills, and communications skills.

Schooling beyond twelve years is already the norm. Nearly two thirds of high school graduates continue learning in college or trade school. Even though most must feel discouraged by the financial burden loaded on at the beginning of a career, they do the work and complete their program. They know their own success will be more likely with more education.

This norm, more years, is important because it means the value of additional investment in education is already recognized by the majority. Expectation of return on investment on a full four years or more (beyond secondary school) is already mainstream thinking. Not yet fully mainstream apparently, is the value to the economy and nation as a whole. An educated population is an asset critical for future success, but it requires investment for its development. Not intentionally, but effectively, we ration funds for learning by forcing young people to make a financially risky decision, whether to assume debt, very early in their adult life. The other thing we do is rush them a bit in making that decision.

Americans would be better prepared, less burdened, and the American economy would be more competitive if the personal debt inhibitor was removed. Acknowledging four years beyond high school as the norm and making it officially the norm by publicly funding it is a doable course adjustment away from the danger ahead.

Slowing the pace for that additional education might enhance the payoff, too. Some people, maybe most of us, do better if we take a break after completing a task before plunging into the next one. If the additional four years of academic or vocational training could be taken at any time during a six- or eight-year window, for example, many would benefit because they would more likely end up in a field of study that was the right one. They would make the choice when they're ready, when they've had a bit longer to discover who they are.

No doubt there will be pushback against what is a very significant change of policy, a one third increased investment in universal public education. There are always a few who will say, "It was good enough for me, so it's good enough for my kids." Usually, those individuals aren't particularly high achievers or high value contributors themselves, so their opinion should be acknowledged but probably discounted.

Some will be concerned about coddling, risk that if you continue to feed the kid, at least some kids, buy their clothes, and keep a roof over their head, they'll never leave the nest. Those worriers have a point. Laziness is native to our species and so is hyper protectiveness sometimes. We don't want to encourage freeloading so should be careful to make sure incentives, in the design of the new education standard, push or pull in the right direction. It should not be a cushy alternative to going to work. Perhaps school should be understood to be what your job is when you're twenty years old. The long-established reality is that school is your work at age ten and at age sixteen, and almost everyone, when you're a kid, except maybe some of your closest peers, encourages and sometimes demands that you do the work.

Certainly, cost will be a point of contention. People in the lower half of the distribution in the United States are getting by on about $45,000 per year of household income, and that's typically for two or three people. This suggests subsistence for a kid continuing in school might be about $15,000 a year. Meals and a roof over their head would cost about that much if provided efficiently. Tuition might add another $5,000.

A bit more than four million young Americans reach that stage each year when, in former times they would have heard clearly, "Congratulations, you're an adult. Now, get out of the house and find a job." If we acknowledged they aren't ready for today's jobs, and we didn't want them to starve, what would it cost to shelter them, feed them, and continue their education?

Age 18 to 21 it is about 18 million people. 18,000,000 x ($15,000+$5,000) = $360 billion. It's not a trivial amount of money. However, remember half of those four million a year high school graduates are already finding a way to cover the tab, so the incremental cost to upgrade the skills level of the near future workforce would be closer to $180 billion a year, still not trivial, but it's not really that much money, either. It's about 5% of what Nvidia investors think their company is worth, and a little less than Elon Musk's annual take, averaged over the last three years.

Important to keep clearly in mind, it is investment, not expense, in contrast with defense spending, for example. It would be a modest number, about 18% of what we now spend on our military, almost all of which is expense, not investment. Essential as that spending is, it leaves behind practically nothing of lasting value other than some developed skills, in those who have served. Some of those skills are transferable and useful in the civilian world.

4. Get the profiteers away from our health.

It's hard to find rave reviews for the American health care system. Anyone who's had to engage with it because of illness or injury has likely experienced frustration almost immediately, often with unwelcoming gatekeepers being the first point of contact. Later it's copays, opaqueness in the of chain of responsibility when a health care provider requires payment and the insurance company says no. And there's hassle before treatment, annoying and stressful hoops to jump through before anybody helps you, the one who needs help. You probably know the drill. You need care; that is what you care about, and it seems nobody else does. There won't be any treatment offered until you prove somebody is going to pay.

The possibility of financial hardship following a medical crisis is well known, too. Undoubtedly, people die early or suffer because they choose not to seek care, knowing the possible financial impact.

Sadly, or disgracefully, some would say, we put up with our costly, decrepit, system even though there are better models we could copy and paste and almost immediately see savings and better health outcomes. Some of those models are already in place for some of our population, military personnel, veterans, and old people. Care through the Veterans Administration gets good grades, and the strong political response triggered by threats to Medicare are indicators that it is far superior to the choices available to those not yet eligible. These programs have a most important feature in common with the higher quality, much lower cost, care systems in place in most other advanced economies, universal access. In most other places, if you need care, you get it, no questions asked other than "what hurts?" There is no demand for payment before you see the doctor. Medicare has only the simplest of hurdles, date of birth. For veterans it is simply yes to, "did you serve"? There are no gatekeepers to pay before treatment is dispensed.

Another source of discontent and complaint about the current system is the feeling that the care recipient's health improvement outcome is not the core driver for how it functions. Profit is. Privatized health care has become a first-priority-is-to-make-money business. The interests of investment firms that own hospitals, pharmaceutical companies whose business model is designed to make as much money as possible selling as many drugs as possible, and the aggregators, insurance companies who take a percentage of the expenditures of the whole system, do not naturally have good patient outcomes and lowest cost to the nation's economy as their first concern. Their self-interest pulls in the opposite direction.

Caught in the middle between the money and the people who are sick, are front-line providers, the doctors, nurses, and other practitioners who usually enter their profession with empathy for, and a genuine desire to help fellow humans deal with and recover from illness and injury. Many over time become discouraged as they discover their corporate bosses limit how well they can advocate for the ones who come to them for help. The expectation of the patient is to regain health. The organization's expectation is that the doctor will see four patients per hour. Less than that and he or she is graded as an under-performer.

But medical problems are often too complex to be sorted and documented in fifteen minutes. Because of the pressing time constraint, treatment will often start as an insufficiently designed experiment. "Here's a prescription. We'll see if this works," says the doc. If it works, great. If it doesn't work, even better for the company or hedge fund or whoever owns this particular medical business franchise, because the ill patient will come back for another billable fifteen-minute visit and probably another prescription and then be sent off to make another contribution to the profitability of the drugstore and its supply chain. People who need care are not well served, the caring, actual care givers often get burned out, and cost to the economy is way higher than it would have to be.

5. Open the faucet for cheap energy.

Ironically, technology that will have the greatest impact to reduce global greenhouse gas emissions can impact markets in a way that slows its own adoption. Electric vehicles are rapidly replacing their internal combustion predecessors, but as they do they reduce demand for oil, and that puts downward pressure on its price. It makes gasoline cheaper at the pump. Adjusted for inflation, it was pretty affordable at the start of 2026. With crude oil at $60/barrel and gasoline less than $3/gallon there wasn't as much pain at the pump to encourage people to make the switchover to an EV. At the same time gas prices were drifting lower, electricity was getting more expensive. Rates were higher than ever. That was true even though other tech that drives down emissions, solar panels especially, were delivering additional useful energy at lower cost than what fossil fuel power generators can. Thank you, AI and crypto, for gobbling every megawatt of new supply.

Of course, mid-2026 looks a lot different. Whether or when, or how much oil might again flow through the Strait of Hormuz is anybody's guess. For sure the price of a barrel of crude oil will stay comfortably (or uncomfortably) above $60 for a while, and folks may again have their curiosity about driving an EV piqued by $4.50/gallon pain at the pump.

Oil at early 2026 prices was already not competitive with electricity for transportation using EV technology available at the China produced price point. Those cars, BYD, Geely, Xiaomi, et al. powered by electricity, are quite capable and more economical than their gasoline powered equivalent running on fuel at $2/gallon. Oil producers in the US need $3/gallon at the pump in order to break even, and the price of crude above about $60/barrel. Anyone skeptical of official explanations of US foreign policy initiatives, military or other, searching for an alternative compatible with what they see, can find clear evidence that a real driver of Donald Trump's wars could be an attempt to protect the price of crude, not letting it crash.

Ironically, the global collusion of fossil fuel interests to keep harvesting the 20th century's gold from the well may have gone out of control. $5 at the pump will trigger a rush to EVs. War in the Middle East and the word "quagmire" to describe it, looks more and more like a possible "dog caught the car" moment.

The protectors and cheerleaders for the old fossil fuel economy know they are in a losing fight, because they know the cost of transportation using batteries charged from solar panels will get even cheaper, roadway miles at closer to $1.50/gallon equivalent. Almost every need for heat or movement, except long-distance overwater travel, will be met by lower cost renewables. It is a particularly bleak outlook for the US oil patch. In addition to the looming destruction by technology from China, there is also new competition on the supply side. Keeping that possible new production sidelined, think Venezuela, Niger, Kazakhstan, has to be part of the story line, the dots connected by the skeptic. A plug in the Strait of Hormuz is a big obvious dot that fits right on the line.

The bigger picture is the huge paradigm shift, away from fire. Fossil fuel to feed the fire has been an important feature, arguably the essential feature, of our story for the last few hundred years, the enabler of higher living standards worldwide, the source of incredible wealth concentrations, the resource over which wars have been fought almost continuously at some location or other on the globe, and the source of atmospheric pollution that many worry will ultimately kill off the human species. Exactly how it plays out over the next few decades is still uncertain, but it is almost certain oil can't win.

With the transition already unstoppable, how would a genuinely smartest guy in the room, an omniscient leader with the power to decide, change course? Surely it would be to embrace the new lower cost technology. It would be to invest in the equipment to accelerate the production of equipment to harvest solar energy and to scale the manufacture of batteries that make that energy accessible for mobility. Ironically, it would be to copy the Chinese.

The smartest guy in the room would offer guidance based on the economics. It would be the path to prevent the United States and its people from sliding farther behind economic competitors.

But there is one other entity that we usually try to hear, whose opinion we take seriously, the impartial spectator. He or she will be pleased if we follow this smartest guy in the room that we just identified. By making this adjustment we will be doing the right thing by our descendants. We will significantly cut carbon and methane emissions, which means less climate change destruction and burden will be heaped onto our grandchildren and their grandchildren. The Spectator will approve.

CHAPTER 16

2027 PROJECT.

The better path.

2027 Project is the course change to pull the United States out of its spiral. The new direction will put Americans on track for a higher quality of life now, and children and grandchildren will be better prepared to deal with challenges ahead. We will invest for them.

The changes will lower the economy's operating costs by embracing, and investing in, new technology that is less wasteful. Electricity from solar panels and wind generators is lower cost, and its use with now lower-cost batteries delivers economical functionality. Electric drive will provide lower cost transportation.

Lower cost to the economy will also result from moving away from the simplistic and rigidly ideological assumption that markets are always the best mechanism for allocating resources. Public utilities and government action to protect us against thieves and other brutes, are obvious examples of solutions superior to what the market, Adam Smith's "invisible hand" can and would provide. We recognize those alternatives as normal. We take them for granted. Now the provision of healthcare should be moved to that same utility model. It will be lower cost and deliver better outcomes. Very importantly, too, rationing of care in the interest of the rent seekers who control it now, will be a thing of the past.

2027 Project will also accelerate the demise of the rent seekers who burden future generations with a greater climate problem. Those money grabbers use every device, legal, illegal, and political, to slow the transition away from fossil fuel. That rent burden we now suffer will be gone, and the savings can be redirected into investment that is essential for the United States to stay competitive with the rest of the world.

The project will walk us back from the brink of the social unrest disaster that is always a possibility when the disparity between those at the top and those at the bottom becomes extreme. Benefits extracted from the collective wealth and productivity of the American economy must be shared sensibly for us to enjoy the tranquility that is the highest value human experience. Those in the bottom half will get a better deal, and we will avoid pitchforks in the street.

Reallocation.

Any conversation you hear or essay you read about the ultra-wealthy, or billionaires, or taxes, Federal spending, or national debt, will include mention of the fact that tax rates are now much lower than they have been historically. Usually someone will note that the income tax marginal rate was over 50% as recently as the 1980s and as high as 90%[1] after World War Two and even through the whole Eisenhower presidency. And corporate taxes were higher, 40% as late as 1987, but now 21%. Now about 1% of GDP is collected as corporate taxes. When Carter was president, it was 2%, and in Eisenhower's time 5%. There is little disagreement that the cost for providing services from the commons and investment to assure the future commons has been shifted away from those who have the money.

Debate about whether it is a fair distribution is minimal. There is broad agreement that those with the most have way more than they need, while those in the bottom half struggle. There is visible discontent and agreement that things "just ain't right." But there is disagreement over whether there is a remedy. Should we remedy? Can we remedy?

2027 Project says yes. It demands yes, because unless we alter course, it will be an accelerating spiral for the country. We will fall farther behind worldwide competition, desperation will spread, and ultimately there will be a blowup. Following that could be the rise of a dictator to fill the void and then further hardship and loss of freedom.

Alternatively, the blowup could be a less violent breakup with pieces of the United States being gathered by other state actors. In either case American citizens will lose agency. A course change defaulted into the hands of those at the bottom will be impulsive, destructive, and likely violent. Far better will be a calmly considered and implemented reallocation, modest extraction of funds from the extraordinary accumulations of those at the top and redirection of those funds to essential investment. Over time those investments will pay off, and we'll all be able to calm down a bit.

Practical approach.

This is a strategic plan. The ultimate outcome will be the United States and its citizens on the path to be full participants as the world evolves to one more sustainable and satisfying to its human occupants. To participate fully we must invest, and it must be investment of accumulated surplus funds. That money will have to come from those who hold it, the very wealthy at the top. They must be taxed.

The outcome and action required are easy to state, but the action plan is of a quite different character, maybe an order of magnitude or two more difficult.

The starting point might be acknowledgement of constraints in place in 2026. First is the reality that all three branches of government in Washington now have demonstrated friendliness to those who already have the money. The Supreme Court's Citizens United decision is the defining evidence. President Trump's unabashed willingness to make "deals" with anybody, and the Republican controlled legislature's willingness to cut taxes, most beneficially for those who can pay, even in the face of criticism over the impact on the nation's debt and credit rating, are clear evidence that the moneyed class is in control of the Executive and Legislative branches, too.

January 2027 looks promising for at least a partial change of control. Candidates willing to talk about taxes, and even the possibility of raising them, Zohran Mamdani, now Mayor of New York, a case in point, have been winning. Editorial demonizing of him in publications like the Wall Street Journal and others that normally speak for those with the money, is a good indication that he is perceived as a real threat. It seems very plausible that the coming mid-term elections will bring voices into the Washington forum who are willing, and in some cases quite eager to debate the merits of this project or something like it with a different name.

It is possible, too, that the Supreme Court is slowly evolving to more neutral ground. President Trump has been constrained, at least slightly, with its tariff ruling, which must be seen as a reduction in his value and usefulness as an advocate and broker…for anything.

He still has power, however, and for the balance of his term a major course correction is unlikely. Should legislation moving some of the tax burden back toward the wealthy make it to the president's desk, a veto is very likely, and a veto override a very long shot. 2027 is likely more a time for developing the plan, not activating it, instead a time for readying the pieces.

The action plan must be fair, and it must be perceived as fair. For millennia, property rights have been valued nearly as highly as human rights. Funding sourced from the very wealthy should not be judged by the greater public to be theft, even if from the wealthy. The strategy and tactics must not make it easy for the rich guys to cry robbery. Also, care must be exercised to make sure they do not feel so threatened by the increased taxation that they will consider a fight to the death to prevent it. Squeezing them so hard that out of desperation they start a civil war, would be a terrible strategic error. Pitchforks in the street, perhaps not, but there would be blood.

The amount of money to be moved is significant, from the standpoint of investment needed, and also from the perspective of addressing the dangerous, divisive, wealth gap. To make the reallocation doable the plan must be designed to be common-sense-good and easily understandable for the vast majority of voters. It should be as embraceable as taking care of the old folks with Social Security and as American as "motherhood and apple pie."

Finding the money.

The reduction in federal income tax rates is just one part of the story of how the government funding burden has moved away from the wealthy and onto the backs of people farther down the ladder. Equally important may be other changes and goodies hidden in the tax code that allow people to accumulate wealth in a way that their gain is never recognized as income. There's no tax on income if there's no income. Financial advisors earn a big chunk of their pay by helping clients reduce (hide some of it) the amount of their gain for the tax year that is visible to the taxman. Tax planning is always in the pitch for attracting new clients, and reducing "taxable" income is always integral to the plan.

If you have money, you can hide money. Some business expenses which require nothing out of pocket, depreciation of property, for example, can count to offset real money coming in. A taxpayer with $1,000,000 on the paystubs might be liable for taxes at 37% on the last half of that million. But if he or she owned (already had some money) some depreciable property, there could be a depreciation expense deduction that would drive the $185,000 obligation on that half million of cash received, down to zero.

A million-dollar paycheck sounds pretty darn nice to most of us, but it's not really that extraordinary. In a few places, like here in Connecticut, it doesn't even get you into the top one percent. The bottom billionaire has a thousand times that. Elon's growing stash is approaching a million times.

If you're in the billionaire club, what other ways might you hide some money? Or maybe a more interesting question, how might you be able to have your money, and use it, without the taxman stepping in and grabbing a scoopful? Suppose you needed some cash to buy a boat...or a senator?

Imagine somebody, maybe Larry Ellison, for example, one of the top billionaires thanks to his long-running success leading the software and database company Oracle, decides he wants a new boat. Imagine a return to the Americas Cup competition. He decides to buy a new racing yacht...for $10 million. As boss of the company, he could just cut himself a paycheck for $10 million, er...$16 million, because he'd have to pay about six in income tax.

Not a very likely scenario, you say. For one thing, Mr. Ellison is already in his 80s, probably past his craziest competitive urges. More plausible maybe, would be a $10 million cruiser, although that isn't exactly a fit either. Competitive or not, he probably still prefers not to be seen as an underachiever. He'd probably want a bigger boat. After all, Jeff Bezos has one that cost $500 million and is 417 feet long.[2]

For the sake of discussion, though, let's suppose Larry does buy a $10 million boat. Would he write himself a $16 million paycheck and hand $6 million of it over to the government? Very unlikely. Instead, he might borrow $10 million and use a few shares of his Oracle stock or some other asset in his $200 billion plus or minus hoard, as collateral for the loan. He gets the money to buy his boat, but there's no income to report.

Accountants, tax consultants, financial advisors, and special fund managers, do quite well helping wealthy people avoid taxes. Lobbying firms should be added, too, to the list of folks who know something about money and taxes. On the list of sources for wisdom should be that last century advisor, Willie Sutton. "Why do I rob banks"? "Because that's where the money is."

The advisors coach the money hoarders on what to do or not do. It's a very good bet they won't be happy cheerleaders for 2027

Project. They won't be eager witnesses either when called for hearings by congressional committees rewriting the tax code with the intent of making it less of a gold mine for the very wealthy who dig into it. A dig for those nuggets might be the best starting point, though, for us.

We must keep in mind the changes we make to reallocate some of the wealth must be seen as fair. They can't be perceived as a confiscation. There won't be many tears shed though, when obvious giveaways are discovered and eliminated. Only the billionaires and their advisors will cry when they lose a generous handout that none of the rest of us could ever hope to get.

Committee to write it.

Hope we agree, there is no smartest guy in the room, unless there's only one guy in the room. The valedictorian, or the richest dude in the universe, or the Pope, none of those are qualified for this task on their own. A committee will have to wrangle this thing into life. Who should be on that committee?

There's one other, not in the room, who might be the smartest. How about the "impartial spectator"? Adam Smith's imaginary character is always looking down, and in his or her eyes, we want to look good. Put them on the committee? Maybe we should ask the spectator to pick the committee.

I think I know the spectator. I've been trying to look good for a lot of decades. Here's who the spectator might pick:

- A moral philosopher, somebody like an Adam Smith, or a Buddhist monk. It could be somebody from the clergy who thinks a lot about right and wrong.

- A scientist or engineer. The plan better get it more right than wrong on understanding how to deal with and interact with Mother Nature.
- An impartial economist, somebody who will call balls and strikes (honestly) and knows how to count the money. That economist should also be good at translating those calls into language understood by the rest of us who aren't economists.
- Somebody who has money. The money person would logically lobby for and try to protect the status quo. But he or she might also serve as the canary in the coal mine. Too tight a pinch would elicit a squeal inside the committee meeting room and maybe prevent some worse outcome outside of it. Also, Gates, Ellison, Musk, Buffett, Zuckerberg, et. al. are not dummies. Someone with money would very likely also bring smarts to the deliberations.
- Somebody who can sell, one who can feel the pulse of the pulse. It could be a clown, a bit like Elon in his likable moments. Or maybe a Taylor Swift, or an "explainer" like Bill Clinton in his prime. Needed is somebody as good as Ronald Reagan at telling a story and as trusted as Walter Cronkite for telling it like it is. Imagine someone as genuinely motivated by the truth as a Cronkite, as smooth as Reagan and as good at capturing attention as Trump. The spectator might not choose one from the latest class of super-sellers. This is not ether.
- There should be someone young and someone old. The oldster has seen folly and might sense it again well before the others in the room…and raise a flag. The kid is in the stream swimming with the other youngsters and may have a better sense of *it*, like whether it smells and how hot or cold it is. He or she might even be better at speculating what

the world will be like in 2050 when the plan is yielding its delicious...or bitter...fruit.

---

[1] https://taxfoundation.org/data/all/federal/historical-income-tax-rates-brackets/

[2] https://www.facebook.com/reel/1942095006347223

CHAPTER 17

SABOTAGE AND OTHER TRICKS.

Not Naive.

If you hope to win a fight, you better be absolutely focused on landing a punch, and you damn well better have a defense plan, too. The other guy(s) will block your shots while they run up their score if you don't do the same. If it's a really serious game, like if there's a lot of money involved, you had better assume they will use every trick, including bribing the referees. Some will even try to kidnap your teammates. If it's money, assume they will break every law and convention unless there's high risk of significant loss, like time in prison when there's no friend in power to grant a pardon. If it's a big-money game there will be thieves all around it, and in it.

We should expect sabotage of our project and be ready to preempt it. We must assume any tool can be weaponized and used to weaken the 2027 plan while it's in gestation, and we should expect it to be attacked as it is implemented. Sabotage is often easy. Just a few grains of sand well placed can be extremely effective to stop a complex machine and render it completely useless. Count on sabotage in the media, including from wise looking talking heads on television and social media, and certainly expect very clever use of AI to disseminate misinformation and to create doubt. Expect it all to be effectively disguised, too. Count on the saboteurs to be as technically savvy as anybody. Digital currency to finance the defeat of 2027 Project will make it hard to know exactly who is writing the paycheck for the lower-level scoundrels doing the actual dirty work.

The Rules. Are there any?

This is a big-money contest. The billionaires have lately grown incredibly wealthier, even in comparison to their predecessors a decade ago. The top ten, all but one of whom is American, now hold about $2.6 trillion, more than four times as much as then[1,2]. In ten years, they've gained two trillion dollars, or even more — because some weren't on the list in 2016. Imagine the squabble if that trillions-pile of money gets threatened with a tax at the same 37% marginal rate suffered by the millionaire who gets his or her money through a paycheck that's reported in full to the IRS. If all the billionaires are counted, the total decade gain is likely double that or more, than of just the top ten. How about a hypothetical $5 trillion gain taxed at 37%? Do you think there will be a fight? A fair fight? Will the rules make it a fair fight?

With this much at stake, who will play by the rules? Could be the losers, of course. Surely some of the big players will try very hard to not be bound by anything. They want the whole pot, and they never listen to their better angels because they apparently don't have any. These ruffians believe rules and conventions are for suckers. Others, who don't even have better angels and aren't even in the game, lurk close by waiting to destroy the pot.

Though blasting that hoard of gold back to nuggets scattered and buried, after seeing it yanked out of the hands of the greediest SOBs might provide a satisfying moment, longer term it would be stupid. Much smarter will be to move some of it around a bit, not blast it but instead, put it to work. To do that, we just have to use some rules that work. Fortunately, we already do. We don't usually call them rules, but they are what rule us, Mother Nature's rules for us, human nature.

Let's build off that, draw out the 2027 Project, the design. Do the writing, and design the end product, as close as we can, to fit inside our Mother Nature, human nature, boundaries.

First let's acknowledge it's a pretty wide band, that distance between the edges of what's normal, the boundaries. We have sinners and saints. We have people who have been injured and some who were born genuinely deficient in cognitive abilities. We have psychopaths, and we have superstars who are also genuinely nice. We have more than enough who are the "greediest sons-a-bitches who want it all." The outliers draw our attention, but most of the time the vast majority of us would be happy, would enjoy a bit of tranquility, if we could look around and see everybody else enjoying a bit of tranquility. The fact that there are now 8 billion of us and we've been around for a hundred thousand years, and our closely related predecessors perhaps a million years before that, is evidence Mother's rules work.

Mother's Rules.

Loners don't survive. At least they don't reproduce. They are the last in their own genes' journey. Rarely do they make it for as long as their peers who live with partners and helpers. Few humans prefer to be alone.

The truly obnoxious don't survive. Occasionally a monster does last and makes life miserable for a multitude of others, but if his behavior takes him too far out of bounds the tribe, or mob, will take him down. If some individual rises to that takedown task he is cheered as the hero.

Leaders of the successful tribe lock up the monsters and also constrain the greedy who are not quite monsters. In the most successful villages, the greediest sons-a-bitches are reined in.

Humans derive pleasure from seeing others experience pleasure. We approve when others have success, unless that success is clearly at our own expense.

Humans look ahead. They anticipate. They speculate and then prepare for the future. They consciously save and invest. The tribes that only looked back didn't survive.

The future usually turns out to be different from our speculations about the future. We routinely underestimate or overestimate danger. We sometimes act like a panicked herd. Other times it's run with euphoria straight into hazard. A few who watch the spectacle, see with the clear eyes of the impartial spectator, or maybe the keen eyes of the vulture. The vultures wait at the ready to feast in the aftermath of the miscalculation. And there are always pickpockets in the crowd.

We gamble, and don't you wonder why Mother has us do that? Apparently, the high from a win is a stronger motivator than the low of loss. Or maybe the losers just sort of disappear, so their hard learned lessons are forgotten. The real winners, at least the apparent winners in the short term, those who end up with the biggest piles of gold, are often the ones who see clearly the mob in a euphoria or panic. They are the card-counting counterparty to the mob's bet.

Maybe there's another side to the gambling urge, though, innovation. Humans invent new stuff. They try. Some brave soul says, "I think I can make it." The gambler: One of them does succeed, like a Thomas Edison, and everybody benefits. It might be that ninety-nine others gambled and lost, trying to make electric light. There were huge losses, and Mother Nature just shrugged. Maybe she approves, or at least accepts, our gambling because it's not always a zero-sum game.

Risk aversion is essential to survival. It's doubtful that many survive beyond about age six without that behavior firmly implanted. Usually, the aversion grows stronger as there are more "ouch" experiences. A fifteen-year-old will do more "Watch this!" tricks than somebody who's been around for thirty years, or sixty years. Some gamblers grow a little more careful with age. Some back away from the table, take their winnings and go home. Some stay home and guard their pile of money. A few celebrate their good fortune by throwing a party for their friends and neighbors.

Those last two, the ones who stay home and guard, and the ones who share their bounty, may be most important for 2027 Project. The former is scared and might help us scare some of his peers. The latter, the good fortune celebrating gambler embracing a brighter speculation, might be effective for welcoming other peers, including some of the frightened ones into this tent.

Laws and tricks.

Our side will obey the laws as written, but trickery shouldn't be off the table. This is a game of survival, so every trick or leverage we have, we must use. That includes any pot of gold made available by a successful gambler who recognizes the moment and joins our effort. The wealthy can easily buy leverage, and they do. They buy trickery which can be powerful but ultimately can't overpower Mother Nature's laws. We align with nature, and if we buy some gold leveraged trickery and use the two forces together, our side can win. In the short term the win will be putting the plan in place. We start by writing it in 2027. Implementation will start in 2029, and the really big win for America will follow.

Human error.

Billionaires are human, too. They can't ignore Mother Nature indefinitely, nor are all of them insensitive to the impartial spectator's gaze. They can be embarrassed and they can be frightened. When they're threatened with higher taxes a few run away, but most don't. Recently Sergey Brin, co-founder of Google (Alphabet), moved to avoid the possibility of having to pay a wealth tax in California. It's doubtful his approval ratings improved as a result. The guy has a net worth of $250 billion, and should the proposed law be approved by voters, he would have to give up 1% of that each year for five years.

Jeff Bezos drew attention to himself a couple years ago by moving to Florida from Washington State. He saves over $600 million a year in capital gains taxes that he would probably otherwise have to pay to the State of Washington. The move most likely didn't make him any more lovable in the eyes of his employees or Amazon customers.

These two are exceptional for their wealth and for the fact that they moved. It may be that other considerations, including that by most measures California is a pretty nice place to live, are why most billionaires don't move. They just hide their money.[3] For Jeff, Florida was also back to home and family and maybe a nicer climate for enjoying his big new sailboat.

The runaways didn't win friends. Instead, they may have created an embarrassment for their peers. They looked kind of miserly. The argument for keeping all the money is: "Hey, I'm obviously the smartest guy in the room, you know, obviously wise and responsible, because I have all the money, so obviously I should keep the money and make all the decisions." Trouble is, to most people, running away didn't look like smartest or wisest in the room. It looked more like cheapest in the room, kind of like the guy who leaves a $5 tip for the server after gorging on his $50 meal. I wonder if we could be tricky and apply that miser paintbrush to some of the others sitting on their idle piles of gold, maybe give them more of a Scrooge look than mature genius.

And how about the deer in the headlights look? Do you wonder if there might have been that moment for Elon Musk in the middle of his DOGE attempted take down of half the government…when the market took down the price of his Tesla stock. Can you imagine the face in the mirror three months into the rampage when he realized he'd lost $100 billion. He might have been the smartest guy in the room, his bathroom, but I bet he didn't look like the most confident guy in the room. Worried, worried, man was probably closer. He likely had also been feeling the bad vibes from the DOGE thing going stale and knew in his gut the Trump stage was crowded. If push came to shove, the president's guards would make sure Elon was the one to get shoved off. The "holy crap" look, or "crap scared out of him" look wasn't becoming. It isn't attractive for any billionaire.

Embarrassed or scared, or both, we all have our moments. The biggest bag of money can't guarantee shelter from the experience. In fact, a big bag of money can almost guarantee periods of worry. If you have a bag, protecting it can occupy your day...and night. You rightly should be afraid someone is lurking close by, waiting for your inattentive moment, to grab and run. You know, too, there are some thieves who would put a knife in your back and laugh as they leave you bleeding to death.

Can you imagine there are some billionaires not worthy of the knife, genuinely good people who might be recognized and rescued by the mob after the bag snatch but before the blood? Might there be some others, though not so good, who see and fear the possible disaster coming and who might help negotiate 2027 and avoid the disaster? They would be the smartest by responding to that risk avoidance Mother Nature rule. Could there be somebody with $100 billion who realizes he can make a $2 billion insurance payment to turn 2027 Project into law, then pay 20% in taxes going forward, still have $75 billion plus...and start sleeping at night?

FUD, (fear, uncertainty, and doubt) motivates. On that stage behind Donald Trump for his second term inauguration was a lineup of the wealthiest in the country. They had all accepted the invitation to be there and made a token contribution of money for the celebration. The mood on that stage, at least from photos, wasn't celebratory, however. There had to be, and it looked like there was uncertainty and doubt on their faces. Chaos was the consistent experience during Trump's first term, and anybody who's followed the man for more than a week knows to doubt the sincerity of anything he says or the truth of any picture he paints.

Those guys on the stage are each guarding a pile of gold of at least $200 billion. Fear of the real possibility that Chaos Man might scatter or vaporize their pile is consistent with our human, ancient, survival, risk-aversion mandate. Since the start of the president's term, the treatment of anyone who hasn't bowed down to him or caved to his extortions is clear evidence the fear is well placed.

A third of the way in, however, there are signs of lame-duckery. His polling numbers are well below long-term survival levels. Off-year elections have gone consistently opposite his preferences, and even the Supreme Court has ruled against him. He has shown a willingness to shoot people, and try, with some success, to take down some of the world's bullies, usually the weaker ones. A few observers believe even that is more for diversion of attention than anything else. He did manage to kill a barely-hanging-on 86-year-old dictator in Iran. Or maybe it was his Lieutenant Netanyahu who deserves credit. Could be the other way around, Netanyahu's Lieutenant Trump who made the score.

This president hasn't won new friends, and former American allies have mostly distanced themselves from his questionable adventures. Even his MAGA movement has weakened. Its temporary friends, particularly young men and Hispanic voters have in significant numbers realized they made a mistake with their 2024 vote. As chaotic as ever, but maybe not quite as fear inspiring, and maybe quite a bit less fear inspiring he'll be after the November 2026 elections, it could be Trump won't be as scary compared to other things illuminated as 2027 Project takes shape. Stuff has been broken and more will be before he's gone. It is scary and must be especially so for those who have a lot at risk. The billionaires are on the careening bus, and for them survival has meant not getting thrown off and run over. But now certainly, some of the riders are hearing the other warning from the prudent voice from within, steady and clear, saying, “Jump off before the crash.” Game plan for our 2027 Project should include amplification of that voice at every opportunity.

CHAPTER 18

THE BIG PICTURE.

Investment.

Discovery follows investment. Every nugget found on the trail required somebody's investment of time and energy to walk the trail. Our modern-world benefits that we take for granted, comfort and convenience that our predecessors of even a couple hundred years ago could not have imagined, like automatic heating systems with programmable thermostats, instant direct communications with any other person who will answer…anywhere on the globe, and the ability to travel to the other side of the globe in not much more than half a day, are amazing by human historical standards. We are served because our recent predecessors put some of the excess produced by their hard work aside and used it to build something for the future, rather than consuming it in that moment. They invested. They invested a lot in what we call public goods, too, highways and bridges, and the education of their kids.

Unfortunately, the United States is not on the best path for payoffs in the future. Two errors in our thinking keep our level of real investment below what is needed to capture the benefits presented by our quickly improving understanding of our physical world. We're not building the machines and infrastructure that we should. We underinvest because we are confused about the difference in meaning between the words investment and speculation. Investment requires patience, an attention span longer than a diurnal cycle and longer than a fiscal quarter. Investment doesn't happen with antsy money. Too much of the money is now in speculator hands, the hands of gamblers who have no interest in real investments, even ones that have high probable future returns.

Our other mistake has been to put too much of the money into the hands of those at the other end of the risk aversion spectrum. Too much is in the piles of the wealthiest, the billionaires who hoard rather than invest. They sit comfortably and are too risk averse. Their stacks of gold aren't working.

Adding to our failure as stewards for our descendants' future is the fact that competitors are investing. They have been and are investing surpluses to produce future productivity gains. The payoff has been rapidly rising market share and higher standards of living relative to that of Americans. We slide back as they advance. China is the obvious exhibit one.

Dangerous disparity.

Throughout history there are examples of social disintegration and the end of an empire or nation triggered by unfairness or sense of unfairness in the established order. Kings have been overthrown, ethnic minorities and sometimes even ethnic majorities suppressed by ruling elites have rebelled and established a new order...after mass destruction and death.

Extreme disparity of wealth is dangerous because it's not a peacefully-self-correcting condition. Ultimately the poor in the middle step aside or join when the those at the desperately poor end conclude a rampage of destruction is their only path. Unfairness is dangerous. Perception of fairness is essential for any society's long-term viability. Americans know wealth inequality is significantly greater than it has been, and it is perceived as unfair. A productive worker might earn $100,000 a year for thirty years, $3 million for a career, or $2 million after taxes. Among the wealthy some have a thousand times that or ten thousand times that. The wealthiest ten billionaires have more than one hundred thousand times as much as the lifetime take-home pay of the honest, hard-working average American.

Self-inflicted wound: Pay rent.

Economists call the phenomenon rent, an excess payment for which no additional value is received in return. The rent taker gets a slice simply because he can. There are two rent takers we should cast off. They drag our economy. Energy costs more than it would have to because suppliers of energy from the old paradigm have captured government and used it to delay adoption of the lower cost replacement. High energy consumption is integral to our modern world, but that energy does not have to come from the combustion of carbon fuels. Electricity from renewable sources is now cheaper, and when other newer technologies, like LED lights and electric drive motors and batteries in cars, use that renewable source electricity, the cost of the service they deliver is significantly lower. 25% less expenditure for hugely expensive essential services is within easy reach. If we don't simply grab it off the shelf and use it, we are choosing to make a 25% rent payment.

Our even greater rent payment loss is for health care. 18% of our $30 trillion dollars gross domestic product goes to a health care system that delivers mediocre-at-best results. Most other countries enjoy better outcomes and pay only 10% of GDP. That 8% difference is $2.4 trillion more each year than we should be paying. We hand over to the rent takers who have attached themselves to this system, or built this system, an extra $7,000 a year for every man, woman, and child in this country, every year.

One other factor...to be fair.

Health insurance companies that act as gatekeepers and add a significant cost component certainly fit the rent taker identity, but they are not solely to blame for the country's health cost handicap. Adding in the mostly higher prices we pay for medications doesn't complete the picture, either. Americans' costs are higher partly because they need more care. Some of the blame for that is deserved by another not so obvious villain, our not-healthy food supply. Our grocery shelves are making us sick.

Chronic conditions, like obesity, diabetes, and liver disease are at near epidemic levels. People with these maladies require care. Unfortunately, they will likely load the health care system with higher costs for rest of their lives.

Recent better understanding of nutrition, the gut biome, and what is good for us and what is bad for us, has revealed opportunities to prevent, and in very many cases reverse conditions that would otherwise continue to burden individuals and the health care system. Cleaning up the grocery shelf may have high potential return on investment.

Climate.

The world as we've known it, the thin skin of the earth that fragile humans inhabit, has always been 59 degrees Fahrenheit, but it is now getting warmer. It best not warm very much; we don't want 69 degrees. Nobody would survive. Of course, people are fine when the air around them is that, in fact seventy-five is about perfect for most of us. Like so many things we measure, there is a range for what is habitable. Some live where the temperature occasionally drops to a hundred degrees below the average. At the other end, humans don't inhabit any place where the temperature day and night is even fifty degrees above that fifty-nine degree mean, 109°F. Doubtful few could even survive daytime spikes to 130°. There will be spikes, a lot more of them in a lot more places if the warming reaches even 3° Celsius, about 5° Fahrenheit above what it has always been for our species.

Students of this rising temperature phenomenon, the ones who do the numbers, after reading the numbers, say we are on track to blow right through 2°C by the end of this century. Some warn it could be 3°C. These are projections of course, predictions of what is to come. It is a calculation, but one much more studied than the one you would expect from a vacationer in Vegas, relaxed from a bit of booze and sitting at the blackjack table. This isn't the random number gambler making a prediction. It is the sober card-counters telling us it's going to get dangerously hot, unless we change course.

The most important number is the amount of carbon dioxide in the air. It has been measured directly on Mauna Loa in Hawaii for the last 65 plus years, and the number has increased over time as expected. Expected is because during that time period the amount of CO_2 added to the atmosphere is known because the amount of it released in burning a ton or gallon of fossil fuel has been measured, and how many gallons or tons have been sold and burned has been measured and is documented in well-kept records. The numbers agree.

CO_2 and methane slow escape of the earth's excess heat. A thicker blanket of either or both together results in higher temperature. There's no disagreement among the counters. The only uncertainty is over how much additional fuel will be burned and precisely how bad the impact will be for the kids and grandkids...and their grandkids.

Students of the problem predict with confidence rising temperatures will result in rising sea levels that will be disastrous for practically every coastal geography in the world. Florida two hundred years from now may be half its current size, and the deserts of the world could be double their size. Humans, perhaps a third of the now 8 billion will be forced to move.

Opportunity.

CHAPTER 19

OPPORTUNITY NUMBERS.

Healthcare.

The United States health care spending is way out of line compared to that of our competing economies. OECD (Organization of Economic Cooperation and Development) published data indicates we pay more than two and a half times as much per capita as the average.[1] We pay about $5,000 or 50% more than the two countries that are next most expensive, Switzerland and Germany. We pay double what it costs in France and Canada, about $7,500 per year, compared to our $15,000.

If we could reduce our costs down to what the Canadians pay, we'd still pay $2.5 trillion but save $2.5 trillion to put to work on other important tasks. If we just matched what the Germans paid for healthcare, our cost would still be more than a trillion and a half per year less than now. To put it into perspective, that's quite a bit more than the annual defense budget. If we just matched Germany, we'd have enough to fund four more years of schooling for everybody who can't now afford to attend. The savings would actually be almost ten times what that important project would cost.

Energy.

We spend about 6% of Gross Domestic Product to buy energy. GDP is approximately $30 trillion a year. That puts it at $1.8 trillion spent on gasoline, heating oil, natural gas, and electricity used by households and everything else that has to be heated or cooled or moved, to keep our economy moving. Roughly 90% of all energy produced and consumed in 2026 still comes from the burning of fossil fuels. Almost all of that needed energy, except for long-distance air travel, could be renewable energy. We're buying more than a trillion and a half dollars' worth of more expensive fossil energy. Solar, wind and batteries to replace the old technology can plausibly reduce that cost by a third. The savings, more than $600 billion a year, would be triple the cost of more education for everybody.

Margin of error.

The numbers here are speculative, of course. This writer has been pleasantly surprised by growth rates recently for EV adoption and the scale of new installations of solar electricity generating capacity. The news has been good from China and India, and despite the efforts of the fossil fuel industry and their advocate, Donald Trump, to slow it, the energy transition hasn't completely stalled in this country, either. That said, a one-third reduction in the cost of delivered energy may be a stretch simply because delivered to your meter, each kWh of electricity comes with a large fee to cover the costs of its journey from the generator to you. Half the rate you pay is for delivery, something you'd get billed for even if the cost of generating that kWh was zero. If a natural gas generator produces electricity for $.10/kWh and delivery is an additional $.10/kWh, you pay $.20/kWh. Grid scale solar might produce electricity at $.05/kWh, but for those cheap electrons used to power your house, you'd still have to pay the ten cents delivery, making it $.15 total. Your power bill would be a fourth less, not a third.

At the other end of this speculation, why should hitting the OECD middle number of the health care cost distribution not be considered as a target for savings after universal access without gatekeepers has been implemented? If we just hit the middle, the savings would be $2.5 trillion a year.

To disarm the critics and comfort the skeptics, how about considering a range of possibilities, like from half the expected benefit all the way up to double the benefit? On the low end we'd have clean energy technology give us a modest $300 billion a year bump and we'd get just $750 billion by copying how the rest of the world provides health care. If we're all-in optimistic it would be $1.2 trillion energy savings and $3 trillion from improved health care. That range is from about six times as much as we need to divert to educate our kids so they can compete with all the other educated kids in the rest of the world, using the doubter's calculation, or twenty-three times as much with the optimist's numbers. There should be a whole lot of money left over. Maybe even enough for a tax cut? 2027 Project wouldn't object if the bottom 90% got some relief.

How much if not quite as much to the top?

This essay is an almost endless string of questions. The toughest one, or almost toughest one is saved for last. How much should the billionaires get? How big a pile should we agree to protect? Remember, we decide, because if we don't protect, the pile goes away, up in smoke or snatched away by more clever or more nasty thieves.

We have reference points. For example, the median wage worker, everybody who gets a paycheck and a W-2, contributes about 25% to the common pot.[2] They keep 75%.

There are historical references, too. At the start of Ronald Reagan's first term as president the top marginal Federal Income Tax rate was 70%. At the start of his second term, it was 50% and at the end, 28%.

In other countries people pay taxes, too. The median effective rate in Canada, France and Germany is about 40%, a little more in France and a bit less in Germany. Mexican workers pay less, probably closer to 20%.[3]

To make the math easy, suppose the number for the billionaires was 20%, that is they get to keep, and we protect, 80% of what they attract to their pot of gold. The other 20% goes to the common pot. It's probably a fool's errand to say what exactly the "fair" number is, and what we should choose as a target. The number must also be doable. For the sake of ease with the math, let's assume a 20% effective tax rate is doable. How much would flow to the common pot and join what we've gained with our smarter energy choice and saner new health care system?

We're back to speculating again with this question. We have some historical data, how much the wealthiest Americans, say the top one-tenth of one percent have accumulated over the last five years, for example. We can calculate an average for those years, but there's no assurance the next five years will be the same. We have to assume a number.

The wealthiest few saw their net worth double from about $12 trillion to almost $25 trillion from 2020 to 2025,[4] $2.6 trillion a year, and little of that gain was taxed because it wasn't recognized as income.

So, suppose we estimate that there wasn't any tax collected on two and a half trillion. Again, admittedly it is a pretty rough approximation, a simplification for the sake of simple math. 20% of $2.5 trillion equals $500 billion. Maybe it is what those richest folks ought to contribute each year to get them closer to what the rest of us pay every year.

Add it up.

What's the bottom line? There's a lot of money here, and it would come from reduced waste and from the top, not out of your pocket or mine. We're the worker bees, and we don't have much in our pockets. The numbers above aren't fantasy, and the middle of that margin of error range above is very defensible. Let's answer the question using those numbers.

The bottom line:

Lower energy cost.	Savings...$600 billion/year
Lower cost health care.	Savings...$2,500 billion/year
Share from the wealthy	Income...$500 billion/year

Total for investment: $3,600 billion/year

To put it into perspective, for $180 billion a year we can make sure everybody gets another four years of preparation if they want it. Call it training or education, or your job when you're a young adult. Exactly what name we give it doesn't matter. What does matter is that the future will belong even more then than now, to those with more brain than brawn. That means more school.

---

[1] https://www.oecd.org/en/publications/health-at-a-glance-2025_8f9e3f98-en.html

[2] Net Worth Held by the Top 0.1% (99.9th to 100th Wealth Percentiles) (WFRBLTP1246) | FRED | St. Louis Fed

[3] https://www.oecd.org/content/dam/oecd/en/publications/reports/2025/04/taxing-wages-2025-country-notes_16d47563/mexico_0596a773/96be8421-en.pdf

Thank you.

CHAPTER 20

ON A GOOD NOTE.

Sunshine.

There is reason for optimism. The chaos of Donald Trump's second presidency has come into clearer view for many Americans who hadn't been paying attention. Politically passive and too busy with so many of life's other challenges and distractions to notice their country going off course, they're now disturbed by this president's errors and overreach. Unnecessarily rough, seen by many as lawless, immigration law enforcement, and acts of war without authorization, are parts of the show too many Americans hadn't anticipated.

In defense of the president, or more accurately thanks to unintended consequences of things he's done, his recklessness has served a purpose. It has awakened us. Now wide-eyed we may be ready for the serious thought and conversation needed to turn us in a better direction.

Leaders always have critics. All leaders make mistakes, and the wisest ones listen for and hear good advice and adjust. Trump's style has always been to push back and never admit error. The style plays well as a show but doesn't work for leading a nation. That is now clear to those who ventured into the MAGA tent but never really wanted a front row seat. Some who fully embraced the MAGA movement, embraced Trump's pitch and believed he would drain the swamp and fix the world, are having doubts, too. Former congresswoman Marjorie Taylor Green is a perfect example. This is the opportunity for a long overdue serious debate about what and how to fix.

Plenty.

The other really good news, at least it may be news to those who have for too long been a bit sleepy or groggy with fatigue, is that we live in a place of plenty in a time of plenty. Fortunately, too, our place of plenty may be less severely impacted by rapid climate change than other parts of the world. We probably won't have as much of our land turned into desert and won't have as many of our people displaced by flood. There will be costs, but they should be manageable.

The plenty part is both opportunity and challenge. There is already enough to go around. Every American could have enough, not a life of luxury goods or continuous leisure, but life free of most discomfort and deprivation. The challenge is that tendency of money to clump, money gravity. **Money** doesn't spread naturally well enough for everyone to have enough.

The end of smoke.

The biggest story of our time may be bigger than any other story since long before humans even began recording their story. We now witness the most significant transformation in how we live since our long-ago predecessors adopted fire…the end of our use of fire. We have finally learned to take our energy directly from its source, the sun. We no longer need to extract sun energy stored in carbon and buried hundreds of millions of years ago. We no longer have to deal with the logistics of moving that fossil fuel to where we need it, and we no longer have the complicated task of managing its chemical reaction with oxygen and turning the released energy into what we need, human comfort, and probably most importantly, motion.

That we can now convert solar radiation directly into electron flow, electricity, is probably not an unexpected advance to anyone who studies human curiosity and exploration. We do science. The understanding we've gained of the physical world around us has allowed us to invent our way to amazing improvements in our quality of life and comfort. Optimistic scientists and engineers have been predicting for some time that we will be able to capture, store, and use solar energy at will. Now we can.

Admittedly, past technological advances have often come with downsides. We made iron and steel because we figured out how to concentrate energy to raise the temperature of that common element iron, high enough to combine it with a few others and shape it to our liking. The energy came from coal, and some records of that time, a hundred years ago, including images of kids in coal mines, are brutal reminders of how brutal and how mixed a blessing an advance can be. Now with solar panels we don't need coal mines.

Those kids with ragged clothes and coal smudged on their faces tug on heart strings for most of us. Even though they were of our great-grandparents generation we empathize with their hardship. The filth of fossil fuels in those photos is almost physical to us living in a pristine world by comparison.

We still have some of the grime, however, and we probably will keep burning oil for long-distance travel, but more efficiently and with less release of the combustion particulates that are recognized as significant causal factors in human diseases. For travel it is much better now than it was then, and better than it was a mere fifty years ago.

I flew big airplanes professionally and remember early in my career watching other aircraft, first generation passenger jets, take off, leaving a cloud of black smoke, particulates unhealthy for anyone.[1] Our cities are rarely obscured by smog as many were frequently in the middle of the last century.

The wonder or wonderfulness of our situation now is that we can leave most of the filth behind because the fossil fuel replacement, solar electricity from radiation striking panels, or solar-energy-driven wind, is cheaper. There is big money to be saved. It is an uphill push to keep that money going to the old paradigm, dig, burn, and capture a portion of the released energy. Oil can't win. It's the economics.

For the grandkids...and their grandkids.

One final thought to brighten the day. This transition gives us relief from that nagging moral question, "What about the kids?" It is kids all the way out to the 7th generation, because the carbon dioxide we put into the air will stay there and warm the earth for hundreds of years, a declining but still significant amount, for thousands of years. If we stop, we will no longer be guilty of making that future world even more difficult for our progeny. The impartial spectator will agree to let us sleep better at night.

Thank you.

If you've followed this narrative all the way here to the end, it's likely Project 2025 has poked into your consciousness a couple of times. That document may or may not be a guidebook most significant for explaining Donald Trump. Some people close in the inner circle are apparently believers. Some are its authors. But other factors, like Trump's history of treating every relationship as transactional and his general disdain for the law when it is inconvenient, may be more significant. Few consider him an ideologue.

How significant that document is in shaping the current agenda isn't subject to precise measurement. How it would be implemented by a next same-party administration, with the same financial backers, is also hard to predict with precision. What is said with certainty by many who study politics and history is that the Project 2025 agenda is not friendly to democracy. It is a framework for governance based on the flawed notion that there is a smartest guy in the room, and that guy should make the decisions. Not stated explicitly is that measure of wealth is the measure of smarts. Project 2025 moves toward resurrection of a monarchy. In January 2027, we can slow that to a crawl. If Trump loses his subservient majority in just one house of congress, there will be sand in the gears. In January 2029 some of the fog or dust or smog will have cleared, and the country may be able to move on an altered course that we will all prefer.

We are in a good moment. Even if it doesn't work out perfectly or as quickly as we would like, there is reason for optimism. Thanks ironically to the almost instantaneous intrusion of AI and its threats and inconveniences into our lives, and to the jarring chaos and noise from our president interrupting our peace every day, there is an awakened electorate. That will be more valuable to our future wellbeing than anything. A close second in importance is the market. That invisible hand will find and choose our wonderful opportunity to save money, to harvest energy directly from the center of our universe, our sun.

Thank you.

Index

Thank you.

Thank you.

Thank you.

MORE TO READ

Human nature and politics

The Theory of Moral Sentiments, Adam Smith, 1759

An Inquiry Into the Nature and Causes of the Wealth of Nations, Adam Smith, 1776

The March of Folly, Barbara Tuchman, 1984

The Rise and Fall of Great Powers, Paul Kennedy, 1987

Deception

The Hidden Persuaders, Vance Packard, 1957

The Waste Makers, Vance Packard, 1960

Merchants of Doubt, Naomi Oreskes and Eric M. Conway, 2010

Geography

Hot, Flat and Crowded, Thomas Friedman, 2008

Prisoners of Geography, Tim Marshall, 2015

Thank you.

Climate

The Carbon Age, Eric Roston, 2008
Storms of My Grandchildren, James Hansen, 2009
The Long Thaw, David Archer, 2009
The Hockey Stick and the Climate Wars, Michael E. Mann, 2012
The Future We Choose...Surviving the Climate Crisis, Christiana Figueres and Tom Rivett-Carnac, 2020

Technology

Bottled Lightning, Seth Fletcher, 2011
The Anxious Generation, Jonathan Haidt, 2024
Here Comes the Sun, Bill McKibben, 2025

Money

Extraordinary Popular Delusions and the Madness of Crowds, Charles Mackay, 1841
The Great Crash of 1929, John Kenneth Galbraith, 1955
Money: Whence It Came, Where It Went, John Kenneth Galbraith, 1975
Careless People, Sarah Wynn-Williams, 2025
1929, Andrew Ross Sorkin, 2025

www.ingramcontent.com/pod-product-compliance
Lightning Source LLC
LaVergne TN
LVHW022217200926
848481LV00006B/2011